Under Jackie's Shadow

Under Jackie's Shadow

Voices of Black Minor Leaguers
Baseball Left Behind

MITCHELL NATHANSON

Illustrated by Jackie Nathanson

University of Nebraska Press · Lincoln

© 2024 by Mitchell Nathanson

All rights reserved
Manufactured in the United States of America

The University of Nebraska Press is part of a land-grant institution with campuses and programs on the past, present, and future homelands of the Pawnee, Ponca, Otoe-Missouria, Omaha, Dakota, Lakota, Kaw, Cheyenne, and Arapaho Peoples, as well as those of the relocated Ho-Chunk, Sac and Fox, and Iowa Peoples.

Library of Congress Cataloging-in-Publication Data
Names: Nathanson, Mitchell, 1966– author.
Title: Under Jackie's shadow: voices of black minor leaguers baseball left behind / Mitchell Nathanson; Illustrated by Jackie Nathanson.
Description: Lincoln: University of Nebraska Press, [2024] | Includes bibliographical references.
Identifiers: LCCN 2023027624
ISBN 9781496237170 (hardback)
ISBN 9781496239143 (epub)
ISBN 9781496239150 (pdf)
Subjects: LCSH: African American baseball players—Biography. | Minor league baseball—United States—History. | Discrimination in sports—United States—History. | BISAC: SPORTS & RECREATION / Baseball / History | SOCIAL SCIENCE / Discrimination
Classification: LCC GV865.A1 N375 2024 |
DDC 796.357092/396073—dc23/eng/20230828
LC record available at https://lccn.loc.gov/2023027624

Set in Chaparral Pro by A. Shahan.

The most luxurious possession, the richest treasure anybody has, is his personal dignity.

—JACKIE ROBINSON

CONTENTS

Preface: Jackie Robinson's Verdict	ix
Acknowledgments	xxv
1. Mickey Bowers	1
2. Milt Kelly	13
3. Edgar Pate	27
4. Moe Hill	39
5. Leroy Reams	51
6. Aaron Pointer	61
7. Ron Allen	75
8. Robert Kelly	87
9. Roland Hardson	99
10. John Thompson	113
11. Glenn Sterling	127
12. Wil Aaron	139
13. Chuck Stone	157
Afterword: A Note on Method	169
Appendix of Tables	181

PREFACE

Jackie Robinson's Verdict

There once was a time when the passage of a quarter century meant something. Not today, of course. Peek back to the late '90s and you'll find the images comfortably recognizable, familiar, and wholly relatable. Perhaps a bit more flannel than you're accustomed to seeing but otherwise, if you could transport yourself back to that era you most likely wouldn't appear to be out of place.

Such was not the case in the 1970s. For all of the talk at the time about how America was stuck in a rut, was spinning its wheels, it was in actuality chugging forward at a relentless pace. At least on the surface. Up until the turn of the twenty-first century each American decade contained distinct cultural markers that distinguished it from those that came before. The effect was both situating and isolating—where you stood today felt instantly identifiable but also severed from the past, even the near past. It was orienting and disorienting all at once.

The afternoon of October 15, 1972, displayed all of this in sharp relief when a cadre of old men from a different age set their wingtips upon the neon green Astroturf of Cincinnati's Riverfront Stadium moments before Game Two of the World Series. They settled in a half-moon that kissed the lip of the pitcher's mound, a comfortable distance from the color guard assembled between the mound and second base, and the Ohio State University marching band relegated to the expanse of the outfield. A snapshot of the scene with nothing more would be enough to signal that important things were about to occur.[1]

Which they were. As the old men shuffled onto the field and took their places, the public address announcer alerted the still-arriving crowd to their presence by informing them that the next voice they were to hear would be "an old favorite of yours, and one of the greatest baseball broadcasters of all time: the 'old redhead'—Walter, 'Red' Barber."

And there Barber was, positioned in front of the rest, an unruly collection of paper in his left hand threatening to go rogue with just the slightest gust of wind. Barber attempted to tame it with the grip of his right hand but still it flipped and flopped in the breeze, the dog-eared corners of the pages seemingly defiant.

Red Barber—the voice of the "old" Brooklyn Dodgers who before that was the voice of the even older Cincinnati Reds. In 1934 he began calling Reds games on the radio—because who had even heard of television?—in the middle of the Great Depression. There were breadlines back then. Rudy Vallee was singing "Brother Can You Spare a Dime?" World War I was still known as "the Great War." It was an unimaginable world even to those in the stands who lived through it.

By 1939 Barber was in Brooklyn calling Dodgers games, delighting fans of the perpetually downtrodden franchise with gentlemanly Southern homespun turns of phrase that drew listeners to games that otherwise would, and by all rights should have been, ignored. To Barber, lazy fly balls were "cans of corn," a hot hitter was "sittin' in the catbird seat," the rare Dodgers winning streak left him to remark that Brooklyn's Bums were "tearin' up the pea patch."[2] They were endearing.

But they, as well, were unfathomable idioms in the modern parlance.

"This year marks the twenty-fifth anniversary of the entry of the black athlete into Major League Baseball," he began. "Today we are about to honor the man [former Dodgers president] Branch Rickey selected to lead the way. Who set a brilliant example for all to follow." On this chilly, sun-splashed afternoon right smack-dab in the middle of modernity, Red Barber was attempting to pull at least those who had bothered to make their way to their seats for the occasion into the seemingly dark and distant past. "He is Hall of Famer, Jackie Robinson."

Barber then linguistically worked his way around the horn, introducing the other relics of history to the denizens of the concrete and steel spaceship that now housed one of baseball's oldest franchises. Here was Pee Wee Reese, Robinson's old double-play partner, and there was Larry Doby, the first African American to play in the American League. Here was Joe Black, the relief ace of those old Brooklyn clubs, and there was National League president Chub Feeney. All of them transports from a bygone age. The age of Bogart, of fedoras, of trench coats with upturned collars.

Other than Feeney they were men who had long passed from the public eye. Time, and the world, had seemingly moved forward, leaving them behind. Not far from Riverfront Stadium one could choose from a variety of films that demonstrated just how distant the early '70s were from the era where these men reigned: *Superfly*, *Everything You Always Wanted to Know About Sex*, *The Godfather*, and *Deliverance* were all on offer.[3] The Grateful Dead were coming to town in less than two weeks.[4] Articles warning concerned Cincinnatians of the impending arrivals of both the metric system and Grand Funk Railroad were in bold type in that morning's *Enquirer*.[5]

Halter tops were coming down the pike along with four more years of Richard Nixon.[6] And the possibility of women entering West Point was starting to look more like a probability.[7]

After the introductions of Robinson's wife, Rachel, and children, Commissioner Bowie Kuhn was introduced and then stepped up to the mic to read from a telegram by Nixon himself. "Baseball has known many moments of greatness in its long history," it began. "But none has been as significant or compelling as that April 15th afternoon twenty-five years ago when Jackie Robinson and eight other Dodgers took the field for his appearance at first base. Baseball had come of age. It opened its doors to a part of our society which had been wrongfully excluded from the Major Leagues. It is especially fitting that today, in the midst of baseball's most exciting event—the World Series—we pause to honor Jackie Robinson." After congratulating Robinson for his more recent work combating teen drug abuse, Nixon's telegram closed by attempting to connect the past with the present: "It is through such dedication and determination today, just as it was a quarter of a century ago, that lives are enriched and strengthened, and our country made a better place for all."[8]

The crowd clapped politely and then Kuhn moved on to present Robinson with what Kuhn described as a "symbolic baseball honor," consisting of a gold-plated ball and circular handle mounted on burnished wood. It was presented "with congratulations, and thanks, and all our good wishes." Robinson stood next to Kuhn, stooped, head bowed. He was only fifty-three years old and it appeared as if each of his days had been a year unto itself. He was an old man, irrespective of the number of calendar years on his ledger. Diabetes had devasted him, rendering him unsteady and nearly blind. Rachel stood close by, perhaps for moral support, perhaps to make sure he knew where the microphone was; a few moments before the ceremony a fan approached him with a ball and pen in hand, asking for his autograph. "Surely," he replied, fumbling for the items. "Please show me where I can sign. I can't see too well anymore."[9]

As he took the few tentative steps to turn and reposition himself before the microphone, his shock of white hair glinted in the sun. It resembled a British judge's wig. Apropos because despite it all, and despite the fact that he had only nine more days left on earth, Jackie Robinson was preparing to render judgment on the state of baseball, and America, notwithstanding Nixon's saccharine paean to both.

Of course, he would do so as he did everything: with cunning, with grace, with guile. Jackie Robinson wasn't going to take his place in the infield in a big game and boot the ball, that was for damn sure. Just as with his steals of home he was going to do this when you least expected it, when you couldn't possibly see it coming, when you finally relaxed and stopped paying attention.

Robinson began: "Thank you very much, commissioner. I would just like to say that I was really just a spoke in the wheel of the success that we had some twenty-five years ago, and personally want to say thank you to a great captain, a guy who was the leader of our ball club, and who really set the pace in many, many areas. Pee Wee, thanks so much for being here today." He then continued to deflect: "I would like to also say that it would be a real pleasure if Mr. Rickey could have been here with us today but to the members of his family, my untiring love and gratitude for the things he's done over the years."

After acknowledging his family and expressing gratitude to baseball "for the tremendous opportunities that it has presented to me, and also for this thrilling afternoon," he pronounced sentence: "I'm extremely proud and pleased to be here this afternoon but must admit I'm gonna be tremendously more pleased and more proud when I look at that third-base coaching line one day and see a black face managing in baseball. Thank you very much."

With that he pursed his lips in equal-measure chagrin and satisfaction, pivoted and returned to his place within the crescent, nestled among Rachel and his children. There was a brief moment of polite applause before everything moved on. Within seconds the American League champion Oakland A's were introduced, followed by the National League champion Reds. The national anthem was played, the Reds took the field, and Game Two was underway. In just a few minutes it was as if nothing that had come before the first pitch had ever occurred.

But it had. Robinson's verdict on the state of baseball and America was a stealth one—in essence he swiped a bag without most people even realizing it—but it was rendered nonetheless. In all of 197 words he refuted Nixon's contention that baseball had in fact truly and completely opened its doors to African Americans the moment Robinson took his position at first base back in 1947. Look, Robinson was saying, just look. Just look and you'll see that what took place that April day was but a step and not the completion of the journey. Look into the dugouts, look at the coaching staffs, look at the front offices, look at the scouting departments. And take note of what you see. And ask yourself why so much of it looks today—in the world of polyester technicolor uniforms—just as it had back when I wore flannel.

For all that had changed in America over the previous quarter century, Robinson's 197 words clarified that much of it was mere surface enhancement. The music might be different, the films a bit spicier, the styles a few degrees more daring, but when it came to race, in some ways the America of 1972 looked distressingly like the America of 1947. As he acknowledged, progress surely had been made. But how much progress? And why wasn't there more? And why was baseball patting itself on the back for merely permitting to occur on that April afternoon that which baseball itself forbade for a half century prior? Shouldn't it be working harder to right the myriad of wrongs it not only countenanced but encouraged for far too long? Without saying it he said it: We need to do more. Much more.

All of these were questions Robinson had been asking for years. Frustrated over baseball's, and America's, insistence on using him to justify their patronizing contentions of drastic, monumental racial progress over the decades, he kept pointing out to anyone who would listen all the ways both had remained disturbingly the same. The American League had been slower to integrate on the field in his wake than the National, he liked to point out, but even that wasn't getting to the actual root of the problem. Despite ardent protestations to the contrary by men like Nixon and Kuhn, there remained ingrained prejudices within the national pastime, he contended. Prejudices that were immune to his presence at first base in 1947. One only had to take note of what was occurring—or not occurring—off the field. Black faces might sprinkle the rosters but the front offices, the scouting departments, the managing and coaching staffs remained as blindingly white as they had always been, he liked to remind people: "I can't accept halfway measures. The Negro is completely integrated on the ball field. There's no reason why he shouldn't be integrated off it, too."[10] If anyone was thinking of using him to coat themselves with a patina of progressiveness, he was going to make sure to issue a corrective whenever given the opportunity.

By the late '60s Robinson had become the unwitting protagonist of a narrative being told about both his sport and his country that he found discomforting. Both had changed, he'd concede, both had advanced. But contrary to the tidy and affirming fictional tale, both were contentious and oftentimes ugly works-in-progress that were far from complete. And the failure to recognize this reality, and the failure to do something about it, was holding both back. In essence, he was saying that while we might not be wearing fedoras anymore, our institutions largely were as they had always been. Real change required more than swapping out the surface adornments.

He grew increasingly frustrated and angry over the excuses posited for the lack of change. To Yankee general manager Lee McPhail's contention that it was "very difficult to find qualified Negroes with the right educational background for front office jobs," Robinson replied: "The clubs spend all kinds of money, time and effort scouting for talent. Yet they find it 'difficult' to look right over their noses to discover quite a few articulate, intelligent players who could fit ably into administration."[11]

Just a few months prior to the World Series ceremony he had an uneasy interaction with the Dodger organization, which was hoping to invite him, along with Roy Campanella and Sandy Koufax, to have his number retired. He was less than thrilled. "I couldn't care less if someone is out there wearing 42" he told *Los Angeles Times* sportswriter Ron Rapoport shortly before the event.[12] He hadn't been to Dodger Stadium in years and had effectively severed himself from the game all of America considered him synonymous with. "Baseball and Jackie Robinson haven't had too much to say to each other," he told Rapoport. While he was proud of his role in integrating the sport, "I'm not subservient to it," he insisted.[13]

He reluctantly agreed to attend only because Don Newcombe, his former teammate who was by then in charge of community relations for the Dodgers, pleaded with him to participate. But if they were insistent on honoring him, he was going to have his say. He sat down with Dodger president Peter O'Malley beforehand and unloaded. "I told Peter I was disturbed at the way baseball treats its black players after their playing days are through," he told Rapoport. "It's hard to look at a sport which black athletes have virtually saved and when a managerial job opens they give it to a guy who's failed in other areas because he's white." If that made him an ingrate in some people's eyes, he didn't care. And he didn't care for the way Newcombe was going around trying to plaster over the situation by claiming that Robinson had agreed to participate in the uniform-number-retirement ceremony because he "knows he's been bitter about a lot of things," and "doesn't want people to remember him that way." Wrong on all counts, he informed Rapoport. He regretted nothing.[14]

After the event he was clear that where so many saw success he only saw missed opportunity. "I don't think we'll see a black manager in my lifetime," he said. "I don't think that's the black man's loss as such, but baseball's loss and America's loss."[15]

Despite the incessant attempts to drape the Stars and Stripes around his achievement in 1947, to dip his arrival at Ebbets Field in the patriotic waters of American virtue, Robinson would have none of it. "I wouldn't fly the flag on the Fourth of July or any other day," he said in 1969. "When I see a car with a flag pasted on it I figure the guy behind the wheel isn't my friend."[16] When his autobiography was released a few years later he doubled down: "I cannot stand and sing the anthem. I cannot salute the flag; I know that I am a black man in a white world."[17] The verdict he rendered on the Riverfront Stadium Astroturf was one he had been handing down for years. America may look different, he'd concede. But deep down it was very much the same as it always was. And he wasn't going to accede to a literal whitewashing of what he knew to be the truth.

For the most part, white America chose not to register the words Robinson spoke that afternoon. Here, as had been the case since 1947, it largely focused instead on the more comforting, more palatable surface image. The next morning's *Enquirer* ran numerous stories of the happenings in and around Game Two but not a single one on Robinson. Its only mention of the pregame ceremony was a photo captioned: "Jack Robinson Received Pregame Award."[18] The Associated Press did distribute a story that ran in many papers across the country and included his verdict, but not much was made of it beyond mere reportage of the event.[19] When local sportswriters wrote up the moment for their morning columns back home (most ignored it), they often read like this one from the *Lima News*: "Jackie Robinson, who broke baseball's color barrier April 15, 1947, was honored by baseball officials in pre-game ceremonies and also threw out the first pitch. Robinson is going blind and is in failing health."[20] In the *Philadelphia Daily News*, columnist Stan Hochman (who had borne witness, and often wrote about, the travails of Dick Allen in Philadelphia just a few years earlier) remarked that the pregame ceremony was "a healthy sign for baseball to remember [Robinson] and the commissioner reminded people that for too long the game had 'excluded a portion of the population'"—a comforting sentiment that Robinson no doubt would have rebuked for Hochman's rose-colored use of the past tense.[21]

But those willing to listen heard Robinson loud and clear. In the *Chicago Defender* Norman Unger devoted an entire column to Robinson's verdict. In it he wondered why it was that baseball had thus far ignored Robinson's "final question": "Why is it so difficult to find baseball's first black manager?"[22] Obviously, Unger wrote, "none of the 24 major league owners have any of 'that old stuff' that made Branch Rickey famous when he brought Robinson to the pro ranks." Unger recognized that the final sentence of Robinson's speech wasn't merely an anodyne, throwaway line. Instead, it represented the essence of both the moment and the man. Robinson was calling baseball out, making "a statement that may have as much affect [sic] upon the future of baseball as his presence did 25 years ago."[23]

The future remained to be seen but the present, as well as the previous quarter century, was visible to those willing to look. The stories that follow make that as clear and sparkling as that cloudless October afternoon when Jackie Robinson issued forth his final judgment. Stories, one after the other, of the Black men who toiled in obscurity in the wake of Robinson's monumental 1947 debut, which give lie to the sanguine sentiments of Richard Nixon and Bowie Kuhn on the state of both America as well as its pastime. Stories that provide ballast for Robinson's judgment that in too many ways both institutions were then as they had been for far too long.

What follows is a collection of tales told by the men who lived them—Black men who spent their professional baseball lives in the Minor Leagues. Most never spent a moment in a big league clubhouse, a few had the proverbial cup of coffee—just enough for the contrast between the experiences they had and the ones they missed out on to resonate that much more. These men entered a world that was opened to them only because Robinson took the field that April day in 1947. By the time they played—the 1960s and '70s—the ballyhooed progress touted by men like Nixon and Kuhn had supposedly taken place and both baseball and America were purportedly much different than they had been before Robinson arrived. That these men were in Organized Baseball at all signified that of course they were. At least to a degree. But what these men also found was that, as Robinson's verdict pronounced, neither had progressed nearly enough. And not nearly as much as even they had been led to believe.

As Robinson said and so many ignored, the failure to address the racial issues existing within big league front offices, coaching staffs, and scouting departments made the game less than it could have, should have, been. And while we could say that this was the Black man's loss, it is more accurate to acknowledge that, as Robinson insisted, the loss was, and is, everybody's. The institutionalized, hardwired racism that was both immune to Robinson's arrival and outlived him by decades rendered the men within these pages effectively invisible. Odds are that you don't know any of them. But that doesn't mean you shouldn't. And that the game wouldn't have been richer if you did.

In 1966 Larry Ritter published *The Glory of Their Times*, a seminal collection of first-person baseball narratives that brought readers into the otherwise impenetrable world of the early twentieth-century baseball player.[24] But what was it like to be Black and playing in Memphis, Tennessee, in 1973, or Spartanburg, North Carolina, in 1965? What was it like to play for white coaches and scouting directors from the Jim Crow South who cut their professional teeth in the segregated game that predated Jackie Robinson? Or to be called into the clubhouse with your Black teammates one spring-training morning in 1969—1969!—and told that for you to make the ball club you were going to have to beat out the Black men in that room because none of you were ever going to beat out a white player, regardless? Or to spend a staggering eight seasons playing A ball in the Midwest League and even winning a triple crown while watching lesser white teammates annually get promoted while you stayed behind? The men in the following chapters are going to tell you. From their mouths to your ears, this is the unvarnished story of what it was like to be a Black man navigating the wilds of professional baseball's Minor Leagues during the 1960s and '70s.

> I am an invisible man.
>
> No, I am not a spook like those who haunted
>   Edgar Allen Poe;
> Nor am I one of your Hollywood-movie ectoplasms.
>
> I am a man of substance,
> of flesh and bone,
> fiber and liquids–
> and I might even be said to possess a mind.
>
> I am invisible,
> understand,
> simply because other people refuse to see me.
>
> RALPH ELLISON[25]

Notes

1. See https://www.youtube.com/watch?v=0hNF65zWB6k.
2. See generally Judith Hiltner and James Walker, *Red Barber: The Life and Legacy of a Broadcasting Legend* (Lincoln: University of Nebraska Press, 2022).
3. See "Let Us Entertain You," *Cincinnati Enquirer*, October 15, 1972.
4. "Let Us Entertain You," *Cincinnati Enquirer*, October 15, 1972.
5. "You Might as Well Educate Yourself in the Metric System," *Cincinnati Enquirer*, October 15, 1972.
6. "Let Us Entertain You," *Cincinnati Enquirer*, October 15, 1972.
7. "Army Opens Campus Doors to Women—on a Limited Basis," *Cincinnati Enquirer*, October 15, 1972.
8. See https://www.youtube.com/watch?v=0hNF65zWB6kfor video of the speeches transcribed herein.
9. Al Abrams, "Sidelights on Sports," *Pittsburgh Post-Gazette*, October 16, 1972.
10. "Jackie Calls American League Shortsighted," *New York Amsterdam News*, July 14, 1962.
11. Jackie Robinson, "There Are No Rickeys Today," *New York Amsterdam News*, February 24, 1968.
12. Ron Rapoport, "Baseball Reveres Jackie Robinson, but Robinson Didn't Revere Baseball. Here's Why," *Los Angeles Times*, April 14, 2022.
13. Bob Hunter, "Dodgers and Ex-Star Robinson Bury Hatchet at Stengel Day," *Sporting News*, June 24, 1972.
14. "Baseball Reveres Jackie Robinson."
15. Ross Newhan, "No Black Manager in Jackie's Time," *Sporting News*, July 1, 1972.
16. Jon Nordheimer, "Flag on July 4: Thrill to Some, Threat to Others," *New York Times*, July 4, 1969.
17. Jackie Robinson and Alfred Duckett, *I Never Had It Made: An Autobiography of Jackie Robinson* (New York: Putnam, 1972).
18. See generally the *Cincinnati Enquirer*, October 16, 1972 (photo referenced herein appears on page 60).
19. "Jackie Robinson Is Honored," *The Times* (Munster, Indiana), October 16, 1972.
20. Chuck Bell, "Baseball Honors Robinson," *Lima News*, October 16, 1972.

21. Stan Hochman, "Rudi's Catch: Best Ever in the Series," *Philadelphia Daily News*, October 16, 1972.
22. Norman O. Unger, "Jackie Awaits Black Manager," *Chicago Daily Defender*, October 17, 1972.
23. "Jackie Awaits Black Manager."
24. Lawrence S. Ritter, *The Glory of Their Times: The Story of the Early Days of Baseball Told by the Men Who Played It* (New York: William Morrow, 1966).
25. Ralph Ellison, *Invisible Man* (New York: Modern Library, 1994), 3.

ACKNOWLEDGMENTS

The spring of 2020 saw the nation face twin moments of roughly equal apocalyptic proportion: the coronavirus pandemic and the release of *Bouton: The Life of a Baseball Original*. Okay, maybe only in my household. Still, toiling for years on a biography only to have it hit bookstores the very moment bookstores literally disappeared can take a bit of the air out of your sails. Thankfully, crisis so often brings innovation and here, the Pandemic Baseball Book Club (PBBC) sprouted out of the detritus of the pandemic to offer both a platform and hope to authors of baseball books like mine. Largely thanks to the PBBC platform, *Bouton* somehow managed to thrive despite it all and what could have been a disaster, at least as a publishing experience, became something else altogether. As they say, extraordinary times call for extraordinary measures and since I was unable to properly acknowledge the PBBC's founder, Jason Turbow, and Brad Balukjian, who graciously welcomed me into the PBBC as one of its early members, I want to do so now. If *Under Jackie's Shadow* is a success at all in the marketplace, it's going to be because of the support of my fellow PBBC writers as well as the platform itself. Thanks in advance, folks.

It goes without saying, but I'll say it anyway: *Under Jackie's Shadow* would not be what it is without the care, guidance, and insight of my agent, Farley Chase. Thank you, Farley, for all that you do.

I'd also like to acknowledge the tremendous and painstaking work of Matthew Skolnick, my research assistant, who spent countless hours working on the transcription process of the recorded interviews. As anyone who has ever worked with an A.I. transcription program can testify, the results can be spotty and Matt worked tirelessly with both the recordings and the transcripts to ensure that the words that appeared on the transcribed pages I worked with to create the narratives that follow were in fact the same ones spoken by my subjects.

And then there's Rob Taylor, Courtney Ochsner, and everybody at the University of Nebraska Press, who make everything turn out great. There aren't any better and more visually stunning baseball books than the ones being published by UNP right now and I'm lucky to be a part of the family. Thanks for your help and guidance all the way from acceptance of my manuscript to publication and beyond.

Thanks as well to my wife Joanne, son Alex, and daughter Jackie, for . . . I dunno, everything. This is starting to sound like an Academy Awards acceptance speech, and if we've learned anything over the past couple of years it's that it's better to get the hell off the stage than risk being smacked in the mouth by Will Smith. So I'll try to wrap up. But not before a special shout-out to Jackie for providing the remarkable, and remarkably moving, illustrations that helped to make each chapter come alive. Of all the books I've written, this one will always hold a special place in my heart because it comes from both of us. Thanks, Jackie, for making this a truly wonderful experience.

Finally, and most importantly, thanks so much to the men who agreed to spend some of their valuable time opening up their lives to a total stranger, regaling me with the stories that affected and shaped them and that comprise the chapters that follow. I reached out to dozens of former Minor Leaguers of the 1960s and '70s and, understandably, most said thanks but no thanks. But the men herein gave me the gift of their memories and for that I can never adequately repay them.

Okay, I see there's a disturbance offstage. Someone's coming at me. Oh no, it looks like the Fresh Prince. Gotta run. Literally.

Under Jackie's Shadow

1

MICKEY BOWERS

> My grand mom
> Used to always say,
> Take the bad things
> Turn them into good things,
> And enjoy the good things
> That came out of the bad thing.

Some of the truest stories in baseball are never told.

When I was a kid, from 1956 to 1960, I lived in Germany with my parents. And over in Germany we didn't have a television. We had Radio Free Europe, and my mother used to read me stories from the *Encyclopedia Britannica* that my dad bought for us. So living in that environment, I really didn't know any of the stuff that was going on in the United States of America, such as the segregation policies down South and Dr. King and people fighting for Black rights. We lived on an army base and it was like we had our own little family there. If you were in the military, you lived according to your dad's rank. My dad was a sergeant so we lived with the sergeants. If my dad would have been an officer we would have lived with the officers.

When I came back from Germany in 1960 we moved to an army installation at Fort Belvoir, Virginia. And we never had any problems as far as Blacks and whites there.

My friends—I mean the guys I grew up with, ate with, slept over their houses, played football and baseball with—we never talked about Black and white. I didn't really experience segregation until I signed with the Philadelphia Phillies.

It was like I was in a protective environment. In high school, most of the kids were military people. The school was 98 percent white and I never had one problem with anybody. I had about fifteen to twenty college football scholarship offers. Now when I look back on my life, I wish I would've gone to college to play football because I would have matured a little bit, understood some of the things that were going on in the world, things I wasn't privy to prior to signing with the Phillies.

Because when I signed with Philadelphia, some of the things that I personally experienced, some of the things that I saw, some of the things that other African American and Hispanic players experienced, were a shock to me. It was really a shock to me.

The Phillies, I think, took the whole cake. Had I known that the Philadelphia Phillies were the way they were, there wouldn't have been enough money in the world for me to play baseball in Philadelphia. But at the time I was happy I got a shot with the Phillies when they drafted me because my parents were from Pennsylvania. My dad and all my aunts and uncles lived in Oxford, Pennsylvania. The Church of God in Kennett Square, where all the hothouses are, that was my grandfather's church. He built that church. So, I said, when I get to the big leagues my family can come down and see me play.

I played third base in high school. Never, ever played the outfield. But they told me they drafted me as an infielder-outfielder and they wanted me to play the outfield because I had speed. I was the fastest man in the Phillies organization. People say playing the outfield is easy. It's not. It's hard, especially right field because the ball gets a lot of action on it. I did the best I could, but I had my issues out there. I told Dallas Green, the assistant farm director, I said, "You guys drafted me as an outfielder. I never played outfield in my life. I don't know how to play the outfield." But they stuck me in right field and I had problems playing the ball off the bat.

One thing I could do was hit. I could hit for power and I could hit for average. Elmer Valo told me, "You know, Mickey, you're a natural hitter. I know you can go up there in the big leagues and hit twenty, twenty-five home runs and hit for average, and help us defensively." And, Dallas Green said, "You come to spring training, you may make one of these ball clubs."

Dallas Green managed me my first year in Huron, short-season A ball in the Northern League. 1968. One day he wrote on a picture of me: "future Major League baseball player—Mickey Bowers." And that really meant something to me.

The next year I ended up going to Spartanburg. Before I left I was told, "You go to Spartanburg and have a good year and there's no telling what we'll do for you." But one of the players—one of the older players—told me, "When you go to Spartanburg, you make sure you look out for Mickey Bowers because these guys in Philadelphia, they're not gonna look out for you."

So I went to Spartanburg and had a fairly decent year down there. I hit .308. I hit some home runs and stole some bases. I was up around five hundred times and I think I struck out maybe fifty-five times. I did my thing down there, you know, but had some problems with some of the managers.

Bob Malkmus was my manager there. He was a very religious person and he tried to influence players about Christianity, which I never felt was the right thing to do, even though, you know, my family were Pentecostals. I felt that a person should have the right to decide which church, which denomination, they wanted to worship in. He would sometimes quote stuff from the Bible. The way that he acted and the things that he did not only made me, but others uncomfortable. We'd talk about it. But nobody would ever approach him about that because as a player—Black or white—you just didn't do that.

And then he wrote a scouting report that I didn't get to see until much later, which said that I didn't care about winning; all I cared about was my batting average and if I got a hit during the ball game. That was the farthest thing from the truth. Yes, I cared about my batting average because I wanted to make sure that I was performing at a level where I could advance myself; I knew from talking to these older players, like Grant Jackson, Johnny Briggs, and all those guys that if I didn't do the job, I would never have an opportunity to go anywhere. And I knew that no one's going to say, Okay, we're going to bring Mickey Bowers up to the big leagues because he's my good friend and he doesn't worry about his batting average. So, yeah. I used to write my batting average down every day in my locker to look at, but I didn't think that was a bad thing. It kept me motivated.

The report also mentioned that Dick Allen was my role model. They didn't like me trying to be like Dick Allen, acting like Dick Allen, you know, trying to emulate his swing in the way he hit the ball. They didn't like that. Well, you know, maybe they'd have liked it had I tried to emulate Mickey Mantle, but at the time they didn't have too many Black players that we could look up to. Hank Aaron was in Atlanta, Dick happened to be in Philadelphia. So who am I going to cheer for? I'm going to cheer for Dick Allen. I liked wearing number 15 because he wore number 15. I tried to emulate him, hit the way he hit. I couldn't swing that big bat like he could, but I had a little pop. I was unaware of all the racism that was in professional baseball at that time. I was really a naive kid and I sit down now and I think about some of those things, you know, and I laugh. I laugh.

One of my managers came up to me one day and said, "You don't talk like one of them." I said, "What do you mean I don't talk like them?" He said, "You don't talk like you're Black." I said, "Well, I don't understand what you're talking about but this is the way I talk." I was raised around white people the majority of my life—which isn't a bad thing. I think it's a good thing because I got to understand how white people thought, and they got to understand how I thought. And we learned that everybody was the same.

I think people took me as being militant but I wasn't militant, it was just that my educational background was a little bit different and I think that was a big mistake that the Phillies made on my part and many other Black players' part. Because when all the shit hit the fan, I was shocked. I was really shocked.

I guess what really got me in deep kimchi was down in spring training when they came to check my room. My girl was down in Florida and I got her a hotel room and they told me to be back in the hotel at twelve o'clock. And I said, "I'll be back. No problem." And they came to check my room and I was in the bathroom. This manager, Nolan Campbell, came in my room.

Andre Thornton was my roommate at the time. And Nolie opened up the bathroom door and I was in there shaving. And I go like, "What the hell are you doing? What are you doing in my room?" "I'm coming to check your room," Nolie said. And I said, "I think you better get this shit out of my way before I kick your ass." And so that was another thing I guess, that made me of note because I was a little upset that they checked me after I said I was going to be in my room. I could have been taking a dump or whatever, you know? So I reacted and was called on the carpet for that.

Another thing in that scouting report was that it said that I'd fight for my rights, I was an individual-type fellow, and I didn't like whites pushing me around or telling me what to do. And that's not true. I had a fight on the ball club with a guy by the name of Rick Gentry, because I was scoring from third base and he told me to slide and he said, "When I tell you to slide, motherfucker, slide." And I said, "What did you say to me?" And he repeated it and I clipped him on his chin.

I did say what was on my mind. I did stick up for myself, but there were guys like Andre Thornton, he never created any kind of problems. In fact, the reason Andre ended up going to Peninsula with me in 1970 was because I asked for him to have an opportunity to play in Peninsula. And he never got to play. They had some older guys there and I used to yell at Andy about not sticking up for his rights, not telling them that he wanted to play. He sat the bench in Peninsula.

Nolan Campbell was the manager. Nolie and I did not like each other. He thought he was a tough guy. He was a little short guy. He thought he was a tough guy and he was like a bully and I wouldn't let anybody bully me. Nolie had Ron Durham playing in front of Andre. Durham was an older guy. Hit .262. And every time Andre would get to pinch-hit, it seemed like he hit a home run. And I'd be like, How's this guy not playing? So I would say stuff out loud. Like, "You've got a guy that's sitting on the bench that's a much better ballplayer than the guy you're playing. He's a lot younger and you're wasting his talent on the bench."

Malkmus said in that report that I only worried about myself, that I didn't care about winning or losing. But I was a winner my whole life—in high school, American Legion and everything. And I knew Andre Thornton could hit. If I didn't want to win, why did I always go bat for him and get myself in the shithouse for arguing that he should be playing? Why would I do that if I didn't want to win? A couple years later they traded Andre. The only reason that he made it is because he got out of Philadelphia.

They finally released me after spring training, 1971. I said, "Look, you guys know I can play. Is there any way that I could go to AAA? If you can't let me go to AAA, could you option me out to another club?" Dallas Green said, "Okay, I'll talk to Pope Paul [Owens] and you know, we'll get something done." So April 10th, 1971, I'm sitting in my hotel room, my bungalow, on Clearwater Beach and Dallas comes over and he goes, "We're gonna send you home. We're not releasing you but we're going to send you home so we can see if we can trade you or find a spot for you." That was fine with me.

So I packed my stuff, got an airplane ticket and came home. You know when I finally got released? I had to go to an attorney and ask him to get the Phillies to pay me, because I hadn't been paid. So they paid me and then released me. I officially got released in late June of '71. By that point nobody knew I was playing anymore because I was sitting at home. And I had some scouts tell me, "We didn't know that you were still playing. We thought you were hurt or something." They kept me in a position where no other club would bother with me, would touch me.

By that point I had a wife and a kid and I didn't have any money. And so I joined the police department.

In 1978 there was an expansion team in Alexandria, Virginia, and Gene Thomas, who knew of me, asked if I'd come and help him put this team together. I said, Okay, I'll do that. I was working by that time at the scouting bureau for Don Priest and Joe Consoli and Joe Consoli kept saying "You ought to get back into baseball." I was ready to go back to helping Joe with the scouting bureau and run his tryout camps, but they asked me to stay with the Alexandria Dukes, which I did. We had a decent season, not a great season. Les Peden was hired to be the manager of the ball club and he'd been away from baseball a long time so he really didn't know how to relate to the players. And I remembered something that Judy Johnson told me one time.

If there's anybody that if I could apologize to, it would be Judy Johnson. I met Judy Johnson in 1966 in Bridgeport, Connecticut, at the American Legion World Series. He came up and introduced himself and told me that I was a good ballplayer and to play hard and be a good person. Well, I didn't think a whole lot about it at the time, because I was thinking about college, baseball, football, and all that stuff. And I never listened or paid attention to him. I just thought he was an old guy who was out there not really doing anything. And then when I got drafted by the Phillies, they had Judy come down to talk to the Black players to kind of counsel them.

He used to tell me stories about how they couldn't stay in hotels and had to eat in the back of restaurants; how they couldn't get off the bus. You know, he played in the Negro leagues. And by me not being in this country, not knowing anything about the Negro leagues, I kind of blew it off. I remember when he sat down with me. He said, "If you ever get the opportunity to work with players, always learn something about the player." I never really took that to heart until one day I was walking into the barbershop and all of a sudden I really saw who Judy Johnson was, what his contributions were. You know I actually sat in the barbershop and started to cry.

When I think about it even today, tears come to my eyes. I disrespected that man. I did not respect what he had done for African American players. The things that he went through. He used to call me on the phone and ask me to come to his house in Delaware. He wanted to show me his Hall of Fame stuff. And I was kind of like, you know, it didn't matter. So when I got with the Dukes and I became a coach, I listened to the players. I became, I guess, a player's coach. If they had a problem or were in trouble or something like that, I would listen. If something happened, I'd say, "You could always call me. I'll come and get you."

I signed with the Seattle Mariners organization after they acquired the Dukes—Seattle was putting an A-level club in Alexandria and Lou Gorman and Gene Thomas asked me if I would be a part of the Mariners organization, to work under Bobby Floyd, who managed the club. We became good friends and I ended up being Bobby's coach for about three years. And then I took over as manager in '82 and was named manager of the year that year. I'm still in contact with some of my players and they call me sometimes and thank me for helping them build their foundation to get them where they are today.

It was all about me knowing what their environment was, what kind of person they were, where they came from. Some players you can yell at and bully and some players you can't. I was one of those players you couldn't yell at. You couldn't bully. You had to understand that even though I seemed like a tough guy, I was easygoing inside.

My defense was, if you came at me, I was going to come at you back. I wasn't a guy that turned the cheek. If you hit me I was going to hit you. But that didn't mean that I hated white people. I don't care if you're Black or whatever, you know, I just don't. That was not in my vocabulary.

But God's been good to me. I ended up getting a little tour managing with Seattle. I was named manager of the year in the Eastern League. Got me a nice ring for that, which I cherish. I still have my buddies that I was in baseball with. Some of them have passed on. Baseball opened some doors for me—I became a Ford dealer. Had a couple Ford stores and met a lot of people there. I got to meet a lot of good people. My grand mom used to always say, "Take the bad things, turn them into good things, and enjoy the good things that came out of the bad thing."

And the good things are that I got into baseball and I met some people from there. I guess my personality, if people knew I wasn't a militant-type guy, if they had looked at me and put their arms around me . . .

I guess somebody has to go through the stumbling blocks, you know, and everybody can't make it. I understand that, but it's a shame. Not having the right people in managerial positions can be devastating to a person's life. I mean, there were times I thought about committing suicide because I was so hurt that I wasn't playing baseball.

I couldn't watch it on TV. I didn't want to talk about it. It was horrible. Horrible. But, by the will of God, I got over it. You know, I got through it. But Bob Malkmus, Nolie Campbell, Frank Lucchesi, Bob Wellman—those guys impacted and hurt a lot of people's careers, especially African Americans. Even Paul Owens, as nice as he was and despite the nice things people say about him, he was in that group also. Because he was the farm director and I think the speed of the group is measured by the speed of the leader and everybody takes their cues from their leader.

If the leader's not going to put up with it then the group's not going to do it. At least that's the way I look at it. He was the boss, he was the farm director. And I think he had an idea of what was going on in the Minor Leagues, in the staff.

Like I said, some of the truest stories in baseball are never told.

2

MILT KELLY

I'm not an angry person because I left baseball
I'm not angry,
But some of the things that took place I'm angry at
But I'm not angry at all at baseball
If somebody asked me to go to a baseball game today,
I'd go
I'm not angry
No, I have joy
But some of the stuff that happened in baseball,
I'm angry about that.

I started out loving basketball first. Once I found out I wasn't tall enough to play basketball, I converted over to baseball because I was good at it. I loved basketball more than baseball, but I said, "Well, if I'm gonna get a chance at something, I think I better switch over to baseball." I always had the talent for it, but I nearly didn't pursue it. I came to baseball kind of late.

Originally, I was an outfielder and an infielder. But since I had a good arm, everybody said, "You ought to think about pitching." So one day I was playing in my semipro league and they ran out of pitchers and the guys say, "Hey, we got a guy here with a good strong arm. Let's try him." And that's how it all happened.

I grew up in Phenix City, Alabama. My father, he worked for the military in Fort Benning, Georgia. So where I grew up, we didn't have a lot of prejudice and stuff going on that I noticed. I didn't even know what prejudice was, because we was just playing with everybody. Then I left high school and moved out to California to play semipro baseball. And then I left California and went to Florida. That's where I faced most of the racism.

My brother Robert got me out to California. He was at a junior college and he said, "Why don't you come out here? You can go to junior college. You just have to buy your textbooks." And I said, "That's all?" And he said, "You just come on out here and live with me." So I said, "Okay. I'll take you up on that." And so I moved to California and lived with my brother and went to junior college. I wasn't even thinking about baseball then. I was pursuing my education.

I started playing semipro ball out there and that's how I got scouted. I got scouted by the San Francisco Giants, the Pittsburgh Pirates, the Minnesota Twins, the Houston Astros, and a few other teams. Once the Pirates came to me, talking to me about playing professional baseball, that's when I said, "Hmm, I got a chance here."

And then it seemed like everybody started coming. All the other scouts started coming to my house every day. I wasn't familiar with the scouts and all that stuff, so I asked the manager of my semipro team, Mr. Nate Dancy, would he handle this for me? And he said he would. So they didn't bother me anymore. They talked to Mr. Nate Dancy every time they came to the house.

It was my brother who introduced me to Nate Dancy; that's how I got started on his team. I also played for Jess Flores. Jess Flores, he had a team in Long Beach, California, a semipro team. He was also a scout for the Twins. And Fay Young. Fay Young was the other manager of the semipro team. They all managed a team out of Long Beach. I used to drive to Long Beach every Sunday. We had people on the team like Bert Blyleven and Rick Dempsey, who also played in the Major Leagues. Our home field was Houghton Park in Long Beach.

I ended up signing with the Twins because they gave me the best opportunity to further my education. And because I would premiere with Jess Flores. He had a lot of training in California. He'd dealt with a lot of people that he could introduce me to. He gave me the best offer. He offered me $5,000. It wasn't the most I was offered but what he did, he also offered to pay for all of my education at any school I wanted to go to.

But I didn't know the whole thing, how you go about doing it. So what I did, I told him, "Yeah." I picked the scholarship. I picked a four-year scholarship at Cal State LA. And little did I know, that when I went to play that season—I was with the Twins in Orlando, Florida; they used to call them the Orlando Twins, A ball—I had a good year and they said, "We're going to send you to winter ball." When they send you to winter ball, you got pretty good potential. You're gonna make it to the show, the big leagues. So I said, "Okay, I'm gonna go to winter ball then."

And then they said, "Well, you got to do one or the other. Either you go to our winter ball or you go to school." I said, "Oh man, I want to go to winter ball." And I said, "What's going to happen to my scholarship if I go to winter ball?" They said, "You're going to lose your scholarship." I said, " I don't like that idea, you know, lose it. We can't do both?"

And they said, "No, you're gonna have to either go to school or go to winter ball." So I chose to go winter ball and I ended up losing my scholarship.

I didn't understand why I couldn't do both. Because I talked to another friend of mine, he was playing on the same team with me and he had the same thing. And he went to a junior college called Pierce College, and they paid for everything for him—got him an apartment. I could never figure that out. I said, "What's going on here with this?" And I said, "Oh man. They did this for you? Why couldn't they do that for me? They told me I had to give my scholarship up if I went to winter ball."

We were in the same organization. He was with the Twins. I was with the Twins. But he was a white player. I don't like putting my finger definitely on that because you're not that person who's making the decision, but you know. He was white and I was Black. I could tell you that. It was awful. Very bad. It was so bad I thought I would just quit the team. That's how bad it was. That whole experience soured me. It soured me a whole lot 'cause I was looking at them like, man, they're fair, you know, they're real fair. Because at that time, I had never seen anything like that. But when I talked to that guy and he told me what had happened with his college scholarship, I said, "Oh my God, man, what's going on?"

I said to myself, "What am I doing if I don't make it in baseball? What am I going to do if I have to come back home and get a job? What kind of job am I gonna get?" Because I was just out of high school. And I was thinking like, Man, I will have lost time here if I don't make it. So when I went back and started playing again, I said, I've got to put a time limit on it. I'm going to give them four good years. If I don't do it by then, I've got to get out of here.

When I was in Orlando that season, I didn't experience a lot of prejudice. But one time, the general manager—his name

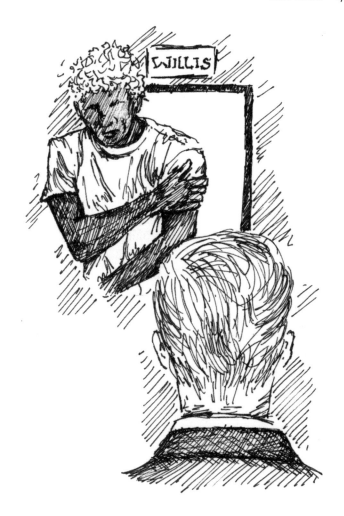

was Bob Willis—I had to go to the doctor . . . I had to go to the doctor for my arm. I went into the office and I said, "Hey Mr. Willis, I need to go to the doctor." And he said, "Well, okay, what's wrong with you?" I said, "My arm." I said, "It looks like I got bad blood pressure, circulation, in my arm. It won't go down; my arm is just frozen." And he said, "Well, how much money did we sign you for?" And I said, "What's that got to do with my arm?" You know, what's that got to do with my problem? I thought that was strange. I was under contract so the Twins were supposed to take care of that. And I said, "I find that real strange, you asking me how much money you signed me for." And I said, "Anyway, you ought to know how much. You're the one that signed me."

I didn't take to that too well. I went and told my teammates. I said, "I went down to that gentleman's office and told him I had to go to the doctor and he asked me how much money did we sign me for?" I said, "That was really strange." That was my first instance of that, you know. But otherwise, in Orlando I had such a good time I didn't even realize how much I was facing. It wasn't until I went to winter ball, that winter. That's where I faced my racism at.

I went to St. Petersburg, Florida, for winter ball. One of my roommates was Jim Bibby. He played in the big leagues with the Pirates. Another was Ezell Carter. We and a few other guys on the team all went out one night to a bar and grill in St. Petersburg. I don't drink, but I'm going to walk up here to the bar and get me a soda and a hamburger. So I walked up to the bar and I asked the lady there, the bartender, "Hey, can I get a hamburger to go?"

She said, "We don't serve n—— here." And I said, "What?" She said, "We don't serve n—— here." I say, "Well, I ain't asked for no n—— sandwich, I asked for a hamburger." And then by that time, Ezell Carter stepped in between us. He said, "Hey Kelly, let me handle this because you're new down here, so you gonna get in trouble. They gonna release you." I said, "Okay, all right then." So he stepped in and took over from there. That was . . . oooh . . . I never had anybody say that to my face before. I wasn't expecting anything like that.

After that, I didn't even go out to the bar and grills anymore. I just stayed in and ate at the facility—on the campus we was at. I said, "This is crazy down here. I don't want to get in no trouble." If I did go out, I went to somebody's house, a friend's house, something like that. And it continued on like that for like two months, until winter ball ended.

My teammates was great. I had some of the best teammates. Half of them went to college and some went to junior college, some went to high school. And the majority of them, I didn't have no problem with them. We was good friends. The coach I had in Orlando, my first year, his name was Jackie Farrell. He was a very good person. He was a white guy. He was very, very strict, but he wanted to see me do good. He and I had some arguments, now don't get me wrong, but it wasn't nothing like prejudice, it had nothing to do with prejudice. He just wanted to see us win, you know. And matter of fact, I stayed in touch with him up until he passed away.

Back then they really didn't care for Black pitchers. I mean, you could tell. I didn't get a lot of backlash about it but I could see that I was the only Black pitcher on the team. And when I went to other teams, I saw maybe one Black pitcher. One Black pitcher here, one there. As far as being racist about it, they didn't bother me at all about that. But you could tell—they didn't have that many Black pitchers around. That was taboo at that time.

And we didn't have no Black coaches, period. No, let me see . . . when I went back for my second year, we had a Black coach—Luke Vasser. But he was in triple-A and he was still playing, too. He was semiretired. He was just coaching and played a little bit every now and then. Other than him there wasn't nobody there. It would have definitely changed a lot if there were. 'Cause, you know, it'd be just like you're going to your father. When you're young you can ask him some things that you probably wouldn't ask nobody else.

But there was a teammate—Mr. Moe Hill—who was a mentor to me. But he didn't know it at the time. I met him in Melbourne, Florida, when I first went to spring training. I saw this guy walking around. And I said, "Oh, this guy here, there's something different about this guy." You know? And I say, "I don't know what it is, but it's something different. There's something about the way he carries himself." And I say, "I'm'a keep my eye on this guy." Every day, it seemed like he was just outstanding. I said, "Man, something about this guy here I really like." He was like my father. He would go to church, he was a deacon in the church and everything, just like my father. And I said, "I want to pattern myself after this guy, after the way he carries himself."

One day we took a trip from Wisconsin to his house, down in Gastonia, North Carolina. And he said he had to stop and call a friend. And he had everything already outlined. How many people keep a diary in their car of who they call? I don't even see secretaries in the office do this kind of stuff. Not this good. He kept a filing cabinet in his car. And then he'd go through that, and he'd say, "I need to call Jim Lewis." He'd go in there, you know, in alphabetical order. I said, "Man, come on, don't nobody do this kind of stuff." He was different. Because the average person, I don't care if you're Black or white, once they leave that ballpark or leave that office, their stuff was a wreck, most of them. But this guy, everything was in order. I liked the way he patterned himself like that.

See, I knew I was going to do something else outside of the baseball when I left it. But I said, "I want to be good at it." I said, "I want to be good. I want to be constructive in it." And I said, "Now, this is a good start right here—this is how to keep your stuff in order." So that's what I did. He was a really good teacher. A real student of the game and a student of life too. Later, when I was doing clinics, I always told the kids, "You can learn something every day. I don't care if you only learn but one thing, make sure that you learn it right."

I was with Mr. Hill almost every day for two years. We had a good time. But he didn't notice that I was watching him like that. When I told him that, years later, he just cried. 'Cause I was like a jokester. I used to like to have a lot of fun. And he was kind of mild-mannered. But I was watching him—how he was, how he handled his stuff and how he handled his everyday choices throughout his life.

My expectation in baseball was to make it to the big leagues because me and Bert Blyleven, we were pretty good friends. And so Bert went on up to the Major Leagues. And he used to come home and we'd play on the same team in California. I asked Bert a lot of questions, and he said, "Man, you got a good chance of making it too."

I was right behind him. I got signed a year after Bert Blyleven. So I said, "Man, I'm going to work hard. Ain't nobody gonna stop me. I'm gonna do this." And so I played as hard as I could. And then the next spring training, they said they were gonna put me on the AA team. I did real good at spring training—I had a low ERA. And they said, "We're going to send you to AA." But on the last day, they cut me and sent me back to A ball. And I go like, "Wait a minute. They said they're gonna send me to AA. Why are they sending me back here? Oh, my God, what's happening?" They said, "Well, we're going to send you to high A ball—to the Carolina League in Lynchburg, Virginia."

In Lynchburg, I was pitching real good but I could never get a win. For some reason, I couldn't get no win in Lynchburg, Virginia. Sometimes I'd go seven innings or I'd get to the ninth inning, but then bad luck hit me. At the end of every game somebody would get a hit or hit a home run to win the game. I said, "Oh my God, man, what's going on here?"

I stayed there for half a season. And then one day I hurt my arm. My arm got weak, just like it did in Orlando, Florida. And I said, "Oh man, this problem must be coming back to me." And I said, "Wow, what am I going to do now?" They took me out of the lineup for about two weeks to see if my arm could get back strong. Well, next thing I knew, they said, "We're going to send you down to Wisconsin." And I said "What league is that?" They said, "That's A ball." I said, "Well, I just left A ball." And they said, "We're going to send you over there, to see if your arm is going to hold up." So that's why they sent me to Wisconsin Rapids.

I didn't like it there at all. But that was because I was being sent down, and I thought that was going backwards. And when I got there, and they put me in the starting lineup, I started pitching and I didn't do as good. I started losing games, my arm started hurting again, and I was losing confidence. They let me finish out the season but they released me that winter, over the Christmas holiday.

I wasn't that surprised when I got released. They had broken my heart by sending me back down, and I didn't really care for being in Wisconsin. That was A ball, and I thought I had passed through there once. Why am I going back? I said, "Well, I'll catch on with somebody else." And I got to thinking ... that was my second year, and now I'm on my third year, and it's getting close to my fourth year anyway. I tried to hook on with somebody else for a minute, and then that didn't happen. Then somebody called me up one day and I went to Mexico. And they took me in Mexico. So I stayed over there for about two or three years.

In Mexico, baseball was fun. It was fun again. Baseball was so entertaining over there to the people; they just root for you and cheer for you like you have never seen before. In America, you've got so much other stuff you can do. You ain't just wrapped up in the baseball. But in Mexico there was enthusiasm about baseball. It was a different kind of baseball. I tell you, it was exciting. And I was excited that I was getting another chance to play. I pitched over there for about two or three years. I did have some problems with the language at first. When I first got there, all my friends that went with me, they all left. But I said, "No, I'm going to finish this." Plus, I wanted to learn how to speak Spanish. So I'd go to the library every day and sit down there and translate words from English to Spanish and then Spanish to English. Just in the library by myself. I did that for maybe about four or five months while I was over there, and I got to speak Spanish real well. I could communicate with everybody. And when I came home speaking Spanish, all my friends was looking at me like, "Wait a minute man. Hey, what you doing? Who is this?"

We won a championship one year over there. And I said, "Aw, man, maybe I'm going to come back." It was very exciting. And then one of the teams from America, they tried to get me. But the Mexican team asked for too much money, so it didn't happen. So I said, "Well, you know what, this is going to be the end for me. I'm going to just go ahead and give it up." So that's what I did. I knew I was coming to the end. Because I didn't want to stay in baseball until I got to be like thirty years old, still trying to make it. I said, "Nah, that ain't going to happen to me." So I just called it quits.

When I left baseball I didn't miss it because I didn't want to be like Maury Wills. He was playing with the Los Angeles Dodgers then. He'd spent like nine years in the Minor Leagues. And I had read a book on him and everything, and he made it to the Major League when he was almost thirty years old. And I said, "Oh no, I can't, I can't do that." I could not do that because my family had suffered too much. I wasn't even married at the time but I said I just don't want that to happen.

If I can't make it in about four or five years, I'm done with it. So that's what happened.

After that I came home and I met a young lady. Her name was Loretta, and she introduced me to a friend that she knew. He was a scout for the movies. And so one day he said, "Why don't you come on over to the studio?" So I went over to the studio and he hooked me up with this Screen Actors Guild. You know, doing movies and parts.

You know, like they do calls. You come in. They'll call you when they need you. Do a shot here, a shot there. And then I got to be a regular. They was calling me like every day. So I started doing that for about two or three years. I did a couple of television movies, but they was low-budget movies. I'd play a Watusi in those jungle movies—a 7-foot African tribesman, you know. And then they offered me some movies where I'd be playing a pimp. But I turned those down. I didn't like pimps. By then I had gotten a job for Los Angeles County, doing construction, driving a truck. And it was a steady job. And they told me, "Well, if you take off again to do a movie, we're going to let you go." So that was the end of that. That was the end of my movie phase. I said, "I'm going to stay with this job. I can retire on this job." After I stayed there for a few years, I opened up my own business, a trucking business.

Baseball was very bitter to me for a while; I didn't lose interest in it, it just was bitter, you know, because of all that happened. And I didn't talk to a lot of people about it because I didn't want them to become bitter. So I kind of kept that part of me away from them, you know, and I just kept going. But once I had my own business, I didn't even think about it no more. I was doing something I liked again. It got my mind off baseball. As soon as I started making some good money, I found out I can make money another way and the bitterness went away.

Looking back on my baseball career I view it as a positive—trying to do something that you really love and succeed at it. It did have some drawbacks, like the prejudice I met in St. Petersburg, Florida. But on the other hand, it was rewarding because I did something I could do and I knew I was good at it.

I'm not an angry person because I left baseball. I'm not angry, but some of the things that took place I'm angry at. But I'm not angry at all at baseball. If somebody asked me to go to a baseball game today, I'd go. I'm not angry. No, I have joy. But some of the stuff that happened in baseball, I'm angry about that.

3

EDGAR PATE

> You guys want a position on this team
> you're going to have to beat out
> another Black person.
> You're
> not
> going
> to
> take
> a
> white
> person's
> spot.
> I said, I'll be damned
> What the hell country are we living in?

Baseball was my life.

I played Little League. I played for my dad's team. I started playing when I was eight. I played in a city called Pacoima. Pacoima was mostly Black. And after that, when I was nine years old, my dad took us to the city of San Fernando to play.

They had a borderline—what's call a wash—between Pacoima and San Fernando. San Fernando was of course the better side. The year I went to San Fernando was the last year they would let kids from Pacoima over to the other side. After me, they wouldn't allow it. Isn't that something?

They didn't allow people who didn't live in San Fernando to come play in their Little League. It's like, if you lived in Pacoima, which is right next to the park, I mean less than a block, you still couldn't play in their Little League. San Fernando was mostly white. There were a lot of really good players who were Black, who were two, three years ahead of me. But I was the last of the Blacks from Pacoima that could play over there. I guess they didn't want any better players, or whatever, in their park.

So there were always divisions, even at that age. But anyway, I got better quality coaching and teaching over there. I was very good and I was big for my age so they put me straight in the major [little] league. And even at nine years old, someone wrote: "Sensational Nine-Year-Old Edgar Pate." I wish I had kept that. I had the same amount of home runs as a twelve-year-old did. You had twelve games total and I hit twelve home runs and that's pretty amazing. I pitched and lost only one game that season and the team that beat me went to Williamsport, Pennsylvania. They beat me on an error. That broke my heart. This was in 1963. It seems like things never were the same after that.

A few years after that we moved to Carson and I played Connie Mack [teenage baseball] in Gonzales Park. That was in Compton. They had more athletes per square mile in Compton than any city in America. You name any Major League ballplayer, Black or white, from that vicinity and most of them played in that park. Willie Crawford, Kenny Landreaux, George Hendrick, Wayne Simpson, Bobby Tolan, Ricky Peters, Bobby

Pate, my brother, he played in the Majors. Dan Ford, Al Cowens, Enos Cabell, Craig Swan—he was supposed to be the next Tom Seaver. We ended up playing together in the Mets organization as a matter of fact. We were a one-two punch in winter ball in St. Pete, Florida. I'll never forget—he was number one in *Sports Illustrated* magazine and I was number two. Lots of Major League ballplayers. Scouts from the Major Leagues came to that park to watch all the different ballplayers. Lots of them.

That's where I was seen and noticed by Karl Kuehl. He was the Seattle Pilots major scout in that area at the time. He signed a lot of ballplayers. Karl Kuehl. Good guy.

I was a number-one choice out of high school—midterm grads. I was a midterm graduate in January 1969. And the Cubs selected me as number one [number 8 overall]. But I didn't sign with them. Derrel Thomas, later with the Dodgers, was the number-one overall pick. And I was number eight. He was drafted by the Houston Astros. But I didn't sign because the Cubs didn't want to give up any money. In those days they were tight with money. So I decided to go to LA City College to play JC—junior college ball. I chose that because my brother went there. I could have gone to other colleges, but I chose to go there because I wanted to be with my brother. But I didn't like the way the coach treated me. So I quit the team.

He was very racist. He only used Black players as outfielders, and he pitted them against each other. That's where I saw racism at its best. Bob Zuber. He's dead now, but he was something else. So anyway, I wasted that year and as soon as the summer came, I went to Connie Mack. That made up for everything. I was so good at Connie Mack and I loved it. And that's where I was really seen because I didn't do anything in junior college because I quit the team.

So many scouts came out, left and right. You know, talking to you, giving you their card: Cincinnati, Pittsburgh. Here take this. Everybody was hitting on me, trying to take me out to dinner or whatever, taking me to these camps to see me throw, pitch. Well, not camps, but facilities, baseball facilities, different places, you know, check out my arm; do the rating of you.

I'm going to tell you the truth: I really wasn't ready for professional baseball. I was immature. I needed to know more about it. I needed to know more about how to pitch and everything else. I should've gone to college because I had a lot of scholarships and that was the worst mistake I ever made. But my dad wanted me to sign so I could help them out with money.

So I was drafted by the Pilots. Secondary phase. Signed by Karl Kuehl. Signed for twenty-five thousand. Fifty thousand was major back then. A hundred thousand was like, Oh my. That's the limit. Nobody ever got more than that. You had to be in the June draft and be number one out of everybody to get that. I don't think even J. R. Richard got that much. He didn't even get a hundred. He got probably something around sixty or seventy.

So I signed. And that was the worst mistake I ever made in my life because I didn't get to enjoy my childhood enough. I could have played another year in Connie Mack. And I could have went on to college and learned from there and matured more.

Because I wasn't ready for what I saw.

Because I didn't experience racism until I got into baseball. It was unbelievable. A shock. And I wasn't ready for it. No one told me that I was going to be facing what I faced, not only on the field, but off the field. I came from a middle-class family and I wasn't treated in that manner.

I went to mixed schools and everything, but when I got in baseball, man, the hatred, the backstabbing, the favoritism, and the racism was just unbelievable. When I first went to winter ball in Arizona, I drove my car out there. I had an Eldorado and they told me, no, go drive it back home and fly back. They made me take my car home. But all the white guys were able to bring their cars and then we didn't have a way of transportation. We had to get taxis and everything else.

And, you know, they were able to get apartments. We weren't able to get apartments. They wouldn't allow us in apartments, even in California. We had to stay in houses way out in the boonies and find a way to get to the ballpark. And when you were on the field, all that backstabbing, all that "I hope that n—— gets his ass kicked," whatever, you know. And the coaches, they let a lot of stuff just fly by.

And there was a lot of favoritism, too. [One of the coaches], I'll never forget what he told us. He got all the Black guys in the clubhouse and told us, "You guys want a position on this team, you're going to have to beat out another Black person. You're not going to take a white person's spot."

I said, I'll be damned, what the hell country are we living in? Then he told us this: "Do not mess with them white girls. It's all right for the Puerto Ricans, because they don't know any better." What kind of message is that? This is what we're hearing. I'm eighteen years old. I'm eighteen and I'm hearing all this crazy stuff and seeing what's going on.

And then they tried to change my windup.

I had a windup—remember that Mexican pitcher who was on the Dodgers way back? Fernando Valenzuela. Remember his windup and how crazy it was? I had one of those. Nobody knew where the ball was coming from and nobody could hit me. But then it was, "We want you to pitch like Steve Carlton." What? Why did you draft me? I never had any Black coaches or anything like that and that really would have made a difference because somebody could have pulled me to the side and told me what's really going on. How to take care of yourself, what to expect, how to do this, how to do that. You know, they had that, being white. We didn't have that, being Black. You had to be mentally strong or really, really want to put up with all of that, but like I said, I wasn't prepared for it. I wasn't told about it. I didn't know what I was getting into. But that's the way it was.

And the coaches I did have? They treated the white players differently. Gorman Thomas was my first roommate. Remember Gorman Thomas with the Milwaukee Brewers? Gorman struck out at least once out of every four times at bat and he'd throw the bat like a little baby. Throw the bat against the wall. All the other teams, their fans in the stand would boo the hell out of him. He was like a little child. If he was Black he would have been released the first year. But since he was a number-one pick and a $50,000 bonus baby, they kept him around. But that boy, he struggled the whole time in the Minors. He never was that good of a hitter. He hit long home runs when he did hit it but like I said, he struck out one out of every four times. Every doggone game. Threw the bat all over the field like a little child. But they treated him differently.

It was like they belonged and we didn't. That was the atmosphere—you're a token. If you make it in this game you're gonna beat out a n——. It won't be because you're better than the white boys. It's because you're better than the other Blacks.

They just took the heart and desire from me to want to even be there. The love of my life was gone. I loved baseball more than anything. They took that heart and that motivation right out of me, and it wasn't the same. It just was not.

It was just lot of things that went on, just, you know, the name-calling. The cities we went to that I had never even heard of before. Oh my God. We were heckled one time in the Midwest. We were playing against Dan Ford and the Oakland A's organization and our center fielder was getting heckled. He was getting heckled by some guys in the stands. So I flipped them off. Well, those guys were in the Ku Klux Klan. Seriously. They surrounded the hotel. We couldn't even leave. There was a caravan around there waiting for us to come out.

It got late and we were hungry. We had to get something to eat. So we went to find something. We were walking on the railroad tracks and here they come in a Jeep, but they couldn't get us. I guess the Jeep couldn't make it over those tracks on those rocks, whatever.

But they were after us. We finally found something to eat. The other guys wanted to then go do other things. And I said,

"Man, I'm getting back to the hotel. It's pitch-black out here." I made it back to the hotel, ducking in and out every time I saw a car coming. Those were some scary times.

In 1973 I got to AA ball in Memphis, Tennessee. I'm with four other Black guys and we're trying to get into an apartment complex in Memphis. We found a place on Elvis Presley Boulevard. There were only two other Blacks in that whole apartment complex. Larry Kenon, who played basketball at Memphis State, was there. It was really nice. The apartment complex manager wouldn't rent it to us but the general manager of our club was Jewish and he just totally went off on the manager and everybody else there. "You won't let them live there because they're Black. I know that," he said. I mean, he was cursing. He was just going off.

Somehow he got us in there. So we were in that place and you turn on the radio and hear that they were recruiting for the Ku Klux Klan. On the radio: If you're eighteen or over and in Memphis, come join the Ku Klux Klan. This is in 1973. And I said, well I'll be damned.

Like I said, I had never been to these places before so it was just an experience. Everywhere we went was an experience. When we were on the road, like in Arkansas, Louisiana, these kinds of places, if you were Black, you couldn't be out there by yourself to eat. So that was another big problem we had.

And when it came to contract time, we didn't get the amount of money that we should've gotten. Every ballplayer that I know who played in the sixties and seventies who made it to AAA said the same doggone thing: Yes, the white players always got paid. They made sure they were taken care of. Then they'd give us salaries and say, "Now you live off of that." You know, you can't even eat right on that.

Baseball wasn't a good experience for me at all. It just

wasn't. We say baseball is 90 percent mental and I see exactly what that means. It's a hundred percent mental as far as I'm concerned because everything was mental, everything that was done wrong was mental. It wasn't physical. Being from a middle-class family, I knew I had talent to do other things so I finally said this is just not worth it to me.

So anyway, they released me after my third year with the Mets organization. And you know what they told me? "We're going to concentrate on the younger players." I was only twenty-four.

I had a good year and I was ready. I was in my prime. I was ready to step it up. So I went to Mexico and pitched over there and pitched a no-hitter the first game. I was 2-0 and then I tore a rotator cuff because I didn't wait to get into the right condition in spring training. I went over there [Mexico] and it was cold as hell. And over there, you get on the bus after the game. They don't put ice on you or nothing.

It was like this is just not meant to be for me. It just wasn't in the cards for me to be in baseball, because I truly can tell you this as a fact: if I had not hurt my shoulder, I would have made it to the Major Leagues from Mexico, because I was throwing over a hundred miles an hour. I was bringing it. But after I hurt my arm in the third game, I couldn't push it to the plate. And that was it. And over there, they don't send you to the doctor. They send you straight home.

So anyway, that's about it.

I stayed away from baseball for years. I couldn't go to Dodger Stadium. I couldn't face it. I just couldn't. It was too much pain, too much hurt. It was a long time before I was able to go back.

But I knew Dusty Baker from the minor leagues; we used to run together and run in the same circles. He named me the Cadillac Kid because I had that Cadillac. So one day I said, "Hey Dusty, How ya doin' man?" I told Dusty that I wanted to come to a game, could he get me tickets, you know? And you know what he said? He said, "You been gone all these years and you're asking me for a ticket now?" Derrel Thomas was with the Dodgers and he heard what he said. He said, "Man, give him the tickets, ain't no big deal." After that we spoke again and had a long talk. In fact, I got a picture of me and Dusty Baker and Barry Bonds in the Giants dugout when they came to Dodger Stadium.

And then I started going back. I could go in the Dodger dugout, the clubhouse and everything. I was allowed to go everywhere, you know, meet with celebrities, ballplayers, whatever. But it was still painful being there. Things never would be the same. They took my love of the game. They took it. And to this day, my brother—who has baseball cards of himself and everything—neither one of us likes baseball. I mean, I pull for the Dodgers because, you know, it comes back, that feeling. But it's not the same.

A lot of guys that I played in the Minor Leagues with, none of them root for the Dodgers. I said, "Why? Because they don't win?" They said, "No, it's because they ain't got no Black people on the team. They've only got two Black guys on the team right now. That's Jackie Robinson's team and look at them now." When I was playing, the Dodgers had so many Black ballplayers on their Minor League teams, you wouldn't believe it. Now they're trying to get all the Black ballplayers back and none of them want to play baseball anymore.

That's why Clayton Kershaw and the Dodgers redid the field at Gonzales Park a couple of years ago. They redid that field because they want inner-city Black kids to get back into baseball. They don't have them and a lot of people are complaining about it now. Now, people from my era, and my age, you think we're going to tell our kids to go play baseball after what we went through? There's no way.

A lot of Black people are aware of all that went on. They don't want their kids to go through the Minor Leagues and all these different cities and work their way up because they know what they're going to face.

4

MOE HILL

Some of the stuff I heard
Yelled from the stands
I heard just walking the streets every day—
Coming home from baseball practice or just
    walking home with some friends.
You'd hear it yelled out of a car
And then you'd get to the ballpark
And you hear the same stuff.
So it doesn't bother you.
You hear it and you don't hear it.
Some people would ask:
    "How do you handle it?"
Well, what is there to handle when you hear it every day?
You know,
There's nothing really to handle.

I was the first African American to play American Legion baseball in the state of North Carolina. In a way it was the same as Jackie Robinson, the stuff that he went through. It was tough, but you know, some of the stuff I heard yelled from the stands I heard just walking the streets every day—

coming home from baseball practice or just walking home with some friends. You'd hear it yelled out of a car. And then you'd get to the ballpark and you hear the same stuff. So it doesn't bother you. You hear it and you don't hear it. This was in 1964. Some people would ask: "How do you handle it?" Well, what is there to handle when you hear it every day? You know, there's nothing really to handle.

The tough part was when you heard it at your own home ballpark. I can understand going on the road and hearing the negative stuff, the racial stuff, and things like that. But when you hear some of the same stuff at your own home ballpark, you wonder: Goshdarnit, I don't think I'm ready for this.

The Pirates had a Minor League affiliate in Gastonia then, and there had been Black players on those teams. And a few of them were now playing in the big leagues. So I just wonder if any of those people yelling from the stands ever went to see the Pirates play, or did they just follow the American Legion team, which was all white. And I began to think that they just followed the American Legion team and never went to see the Pirates play because they had Black players and dark-skinned Latin players on those teams. How do you teach people to come out and be negative about people you don't even know? That's what I don't understand.

I was signed by the Orioles in 1965. The Pirates wanted to sign me before then but couldn't because of my age—I was only sixteen at the time. And then the Orioles began following me around. I mean, every time I turned around there's an Orioles scout in my face. And I said, Well, they're showing the most interest. So I signed with them in September.

I started off in the Midwest League. I played in Appleton, Wisconsin. It was a big transition because there were no African Americans in Appleton. It was an all-white town. There were three Black players on the team. But, believe it or not, I got along better there than I did in my old hometown because they loved baseball there and they didn't care if you were Black or white, they just came out to see baseball. That's what I didn't understand. In an all-white town I never heard any negative or racist stuff. There may have been some, but I never heard it.

I thought the Orioles organization was pretty good because of the managers and instructors I had there. I had Earl Weaver, Cal Ripkin Sr., Billy DeMars. All those guys were big-league managers or coaches down the road. And I was considered a prospect at one time too, which was important because they're gonna stay on those prospects and work and work and work with them to get them what they need. If you were considered a prospect you got all the hitting or fielding or baserunning and everything you needed to be a complete player. And that's just what they did with me. They worked me—oh, man—they worked me. I mean, they worked me hard, which didn't bother me none because I loved it.

I was with the Orioles organization for a few years and then I got sick. I had some stomach problems and during that time they brought in a new farm director who had no idea about the players and they sent me home. I was hoping to get better so I could get back out and play. But I got released before that happened. So I sat out the summer of 1969 and that's how I ended up signing with the Twins organization.

I knew a couple of guys who scouted for the Twins. And when the Orioles released me, I got in touch with them. I worked out with them just about that whole summer because the Twins had their AA club in Charlotte, which was only eighteen miles from me. One of the scouts said that if all goes well, he was going to sign me. And then one day, out of the blue, he called me and said he had a contract and I went to sign it and the rest is history.

So I signed with them and within two years I was back in the Midwest League—this time with Wisconsin Rapids. I had a bunch of really good years with them, but every year there I was, back with Wisconsin Rapids. And that's what I don't understand. And nobody could explain it to me. After my first year with the Twins, at Orlando, where I hit .274 with twenty-two home runs, I went to spring training the next year with the AAA club. I think I played just about every single game in spring training. Had one of the best springs I've ever had in my life. And they sent me to AA.

I got off to a decent start but then all of a sudden everything just fell apart and they sent me to single-A Lynchburg. I was there for a while in '71 and then I ended up at Wisconsin Rapids for the remainder of that year. And the next year they sent me back to Wisconsin. And then the next year they sent me back to Wisconsin. And then they sent me back to Wisconsin again. I was there for eight years. I loved the area but I didn't want to make a career there.

The people in Wisconsin were outstanding, but you know, your goal every year is to have a good year and then go to the next level. And there were a lot of people who came in and didn't have the years that I had but went to the next level. Two of my roommates played in the big leagues—Gary Ward and Al Woods.

In 1974 we had one of the best class-A clubs in baseball. We had Al Woods, Gary Ward, Larry Wolfe—all future big leaguers. And we had Jerry Garvin, who pitched in the big leagues. All those guys moved up. I went right back there.

And I won the triple crown that year. I was going to walk away from baseball that spring because the Dodgers' Minor League director came to me and told me that they tried to make a deal for me and our farm director, George Brophy, would not talk to him. And I got so darned mad that, I don't know, I just decided to walk away. But one of my friends said, "Don't walk away. Show them you can still play." So I showed up for spring training and I think I had the best spring training probably in baseball that year. And then I hit eighteen home runs during the first month of the season. Yet that wasn't good enough for them. Evidently it wasn't because nothing ever happened.

George Brophy was a hard guy to talk to. You started talking to him and he was likely to get loud. I mean, he'd get loud and you just had to get out of his office.

I would go to him and ask, "Why do you keep sending me back there?" And he'd say, "Well, we want you to stay there and help out the young Black players." But that's not what I signed up for. So I said, "If you want me to do that then make me a manager." And he'd say, "Well, we'll consider that." He would say it but there was nothing in writing to say, "Yes, we would consider you to be a manager."

Or I'd say, "If you want me to help out the young Black players, then pay me for it." It was hard to get a raise in the organization. They'd always tell you, "Well, we lost money. We lost money. We can't give raises." But you tell me: How are you going to run an organization paying players millions of dollars and you can't pay a Minor League player? You can't give them a two hundred, three hundred dollar raise? The highest raise I ever got in the Twins organization was a hundred dollars. And that was after my triple crown year. And you look down through the years at the years that I had, do you think I should have gotten more? Or was a hundred dollars feasible for what I did?

I didn't make any money at baseball. I mean, there wasn't a lot of money made in baseball back then, anyway. Even in the Major Leagues, I think, back in the sixties and seventies, a Major League salary was like $12,000 a year. But then again,

I was in it when they started making big money, but I never made any of it or could get out of the Twins organization so I could get an opportunity to make it. There was no five-year free agency in Minor League baseball when I played.

But the thing about it was that I played for the love of the game. That's just the way I felt. I loved playing and I love helping people in the game. I felt that I helped a lot of players as a player myself. There were times, after ball games, six or seven of us would grab a six-pack and we'd all go out to my place. I lived on a lake. And we'd sit and talk baseball, sometimes until two or three o'clock in the morning and have a beer.

We'd just talk about baseball—things that we felt we should have done this way instead of that way, you know? That's how we made it better for each other, because we started watching each other to see if we were doing it that way—the way that we felt it should be done. If you weren't, we'd let you know about it. We'd sit and talk every night, just about—when we were at home at least. Even pitchers would come out. There were a couple of pitchers who would come out and sit and talk. I had nothing to do with pitching but you could ask them about certain pitchers, or certain pitches they threw in certain situations. I think all of that helped us.

Anyway, like I said, I just kept going back to Wisconsin Rapids and having good years. I had five straight years where nowadays at the end of the season you may get a cup of coffee in the big leagues. And there were players in the Midwest League who didn't have quite the years that I had, and I'd see them playing in the big leagues in September, or going to Major League spring training. I never got those opportunities.

And then, after eight years, they ended up selling my contract to Kansas City. I'm thirty-two years old. Where am I going to go now?

I went to their AAA spring training and played just about

every day. And then on the last day of spring training they sent me down to AA, where I played with Jacksonville. John Schuerholz was the farm director there at the time and after they sent me down he said, "Well, we're going to get you back up here," blah, blah, blah.

I got off to a good start. Everywhere I went I'd get off to a good start and then something would happen and the wheels would fall off and I wouldn't do as well as I wanted to. When that happened here, they released me as a player and signed me right back as a coach. And Schuerholz told me when he signed me back as a coach, he said, "Well, we couldn't get you to the big leagues as a player, but we're going to see if we can get you there as a coach."

Well, okay. So I was there as a coach, kind of splitting time between Gulf Coast and Fort Myers in the Florida State League. And I became a roving hitting instructor. They used to take all of the roving instructors—outfield, infield, pitching, hitting—all those guys usually would go to big-league spring-training camp. I never did. All these other guys did.

I was the only Black instructor in the Kansas City organization. They took the Rookie League coach to big-league camp instead of me.

You know, the saddest thing was that there was a lot of racism. There was a lot of racism in baseball and there still is. I saw it when I was a roving instructor. I was a coach for twenty-eight years and you still see it but they try to cover it up with other things. Well, they can't cover that up. You can't cover up a racist. You can't cover up me being a Black man. I'm Black. It's that simple. If you're doing the job, I don't care what color you are. If you're doing the job you should have the opportunity to go higher.

It's not just in one organization. It's everywhere. I mean, they have a Black player here, a Black coach there, a Black player here, and a Black coach there and stuff like that.

One here and one there. Why? Just to have one or two coaches. And they wonder why they don't have any Black players. It's because they choose to go other places because they see there are no Black coaches around and that Black players get treated differently. I saw that when I was a Black coach, listening to the way some of the coaches talked to the Black players.

They get handled differently. Some of the stuff they say to them, and the way they talk to them: You can't do this and you can't do that, you gotta do it this way. And I've even heard coaches tell them if you can't do it this way, we're going to send you home.

That's not their job. Your job is to work with them, hoping they can get better. And if you work with them and they trust you and believe in you, there's an 80 to 90 percent chance they are going to get better. Because they trust you. So many Black players lose trust in the coaches they're working with. I've seen it, but I couldn't step in and say, "Wait a minute, that's not the way it's supposed to be." I can't do that. I can't do that because most of the time it was the head guy doing it and you can't say that.

Players are not stupid. I mean, you check some of the colleges these players went to and what they majored in, look at some of the other stuff they've done. They're not stupid. They're not dumb and don't understand baseball. So don't talk to them that way. They'll say, "Why did he tell me that? Because I know it's not right. I know it's not right. I just want somebody to help me correct it." It's sad. It's very sad. And the worst part about it is that it's still that way. And you look around at baseball, how many Black players do you see on a lot of these baseball teams now?

Sometimes in spring training we'd have two or three or four hitting instructors. And some of the Black players would come to me and ask, "What group are you doing? What group are you throwing to? I want to get in your group. I want to get in your group because you handle your group differently." I'd say, "Well, I don't know about that. I just like to treat everybody the way I'd want to be treated."

As I said, the prospects, they're gonna get more instruction than a guy just filling out the roster. But I didn't see it that way. If you've signed, you're a prospect. If you've got that uniform and you're gonna play, you're a prospect. If they're gonna put you on the field of play, you're a prospect. Play him, let him play, let them play. They played their way onto the team, let them play their way off the team, you know? You can't sign a team full of number-one prospects. That's the way I saw it. I didn't work any differently with a number-one prospect, or a guy who signed as a free agent. I worked with them the same way. Because you never know. You may have that diamond in the rough. I never got that opportunity but maybe somebody else will. If you treat them right you're going to get better production. They're going to come to work. They're going to come to work and let you know, "I'm here to work." Some of the coaches overlooked certain players. They would work with them, but they didn't get the same attention as the other players.

I'd tell them, "You may not end up in the big leagues, but you'll get higher than you are right now. Just work hard and believe in yourself." And that's what they did. And I got complimented by the players, not by the Minor League directors. They'd come to me and thank me for working with them and helping them to get to the next level.

But I never got that from a Minor League director: You did this, or you did that to get this player to the next level. It was always a player coming to me, thanking me.

After I left coaching with Baltimore in 2012, I worked at a baseball academy for five years. And they'd have these teams with players, ten, eleven, twelve, thirteen years old. And you wouldn't believe the Black players playing there: one on this team, one on that team, one on the next team.

I was one of the roving instructors there. I'd pick and choose which games I went to. I might see a game Friday night, I might see another game on Saturday morning, another game that evening, and another game on Sunday. And whenever I'd get there I'd tell the coaches: "I don't want to hear any yelling and screaming." A lot of coaches love to holler and yell at the players. So I'd say to them, "When you start yelling, I'm going to start walking. So when I start walking don't come to me and ask me why I'm walking. I'm telling you right now."

There's a better way. Because if you start yelling and screaming at a young player they're going to quit on you. They're going to quit because they're afraid of making a mistake because they know you're going to yell at them. And the thing about it is when I worked with guys there, they loved it because I made it simple for them, made everything simple and easy to where they could understand it. I would tell them, "If you don't understand something, stop me and ask questions. No question is a stupid question if it is pertaining to what you're doing."

And the thing about it is that when you get those young players to love it, they go back and tell their parents and the parents come and they say, "They love working with you. What are you doing different?" I'm just teaching them how to play baseball as simply and easily as I possibly can. I'm telling them something they can understand. And that's when they start trusting you and you get better production out of them. Everybody wins: the parents love it and the players seem to think that they're getting better. So if they seem to think they're getting better, then we're getting somewhere. And if they don't feel that, let's turn the page back and start over again and see where we can get from there.

Some of these coaches get too scientific. You can't teach an eleven-year-old player the same way you teach a college player. You can't do it. And these other coaches will tell you, I can't get through to this kid. Well, discuss it with him or tell him in a way that an eleven-year-old can understand, not a twenty-year-old. Tell them that way. And you will get production out of them. They will understand. And they will appreciate you more.

Baseball is very simple. We make it tough.

Sometimes I say to myself that I came along forty years too soon. But I still love the game. I work with kids back here, giving private hitting lessons. None of them have signed professional contracts, but some go on to play college baseball and they love it. They love it and they get better.

I still feel, though, and I guess everybody feels this way, but I feel that I should have gotten some time in the big leagues.

I had the potential to probably play AA, AAA baseball, but never got that opportunity. There was one player I remember who had a brother in the big leagues and he was riding his coattail. This guy never hit over .220 but he was ahead of me because his brother was in the big leagues. And you wonder why, why, why is he going as well as he is—moving on, moving up. And it was because of the color of his skin and the coattail he was riding. He never hit over .220 but he played in the big leagues. Hell, I can probably still hit .220. But he got his time in the big leagues and I never got a cup of coffee. That's what leaves a bitter taste in your mouth. That leaves a bitter taste in your mouth right there.

5

LEROY REAMS

I wound up spending a week in the Major Leagues
One week
It was like amazing grace
It was a wonderful experience to play in the big leagues
To warm up with the big guys
To play in the big leagues
To watch some games.
And you see where your talent level really is
If I had recognized
Or understood
Years earlier
What my talent level really was,
I'd have left the game a long time ago.

I got signed in July of 1961 by the New York Yankees, but I didn't go to spring training until '62. There was no bonus—either sign for nothing or don't sign at all. So I took the deal. I wanted to play baseball. I think I got $350 a month.

When I went to Yankee camp there were about 450 guys from deep within their system, from class A–ball down. And so, when they told me I made the team, I was elated. Going to Idaho Falls—class C—where I'd play for two years, felt wonderful because I made the team.

Going to Idaho was an experience in itself, though.

In Idaho Falls, I think there was only about ten to fifteen Blacks in the whole town. And they were old. I went to live with one of the families for a while but that didn't last long. It was just a lonesome experience.

In my first year I was the only Black player for a while. Then a guy came later—Jim Horsford. There was nothing, period, for Blacks there at that time. Like I said, there were only ten to twelve Black people in the whole city. Matter of fact, in the whole state of Idaho, the only places there were even a few Blacks was Boise and Pocatello, which was another little city. But we only commuted for games there, we didn't stay overnight. So it was very lonesome. A long and lonesome experience.

Idaho Falls was not segregated because there was nothing to segregate. There were no Blacks. The whole state of Idaho there was no segregation, but that was because there was basically nothing to segregate.

On the field, there was constant, I don't know if it's pressure, but the situation was that you had to produce. Back in those days, especially being the only Black on the team, you had to play and you couldn't go too many days without getting a hit.

After my second season in Idaho Falls, I got drafted by the Phillies in the winter draft, a Minor League draft. I was just happy that I had somewhere to play. I never thought much about the fact that it was the Phillies who drafted me. It was just an opportunity to play baseball. But there was a big contrast in the Minor League and managerial structures between the Yankees and the Phillies. The Phillies organization wasn't the greatest structure to play under for Blacks. It was rough.

Management, the people who ran the organization . . . you were on tiptoes. You'd have to watch what you were doing. It was kinda like a caste system. If you were a Black player, unless you were a superstar, you didn't advance rapidly. But it wasn't something I talked about with other Black players within the organization. We were all just trying to hang on to make the team.

My manager in Eugene was Bob Wellman. He was a nice guy. He didn't do much, or say much. He'd just put you on the field and let you play. It was more the structural atmosphere that you were under there. With the Yankees, you weren't scrutinized as much. It was like a free society there. Being Black, you didn't feel like you were under a whole bunch of pressure. You had freedom. With the Phillies, it was a pressure cooker, especially for Blacks. And there weren't that many.

After that I went to Chattanooga. Andy Seminick was the manager. He was good to play for. He was a very nice man. I played for him two years. In Chattanooga and then in Macon, both in the Southern League. Being in the South was totally different than being in Idaho Falls and Eugene. You'd have to watch your Ps and Qs in Tennessee and in Alabama and those places. You mostly lived going to and from the ballpark. You didn't do a lot of roaming. I lived with a family in Chattanooga. You'd just find a family to live with. You'd look in the advertisements. The Phillies didn't set you up with anything. Nobody never did nothing like that.

In a couple of cities you had some hecklers. But you just play, you know, you're just playing baseball. That's what you did. This was in 1965 in Chattanooga, the first year of desegregation there. It was the year the color line was broken for you to stay in the major hotels there. I didn't have an issue with that in Eugene or Idaho Falls. There was not much discussion of that in Chattanooga but it was different—the Black players used to have to stay across the tracks. So, being able to stay with the regular team instead of being picked up over the tracks. . . . I had that experience in spring training in Florida. With both the Yankees and Phillies. With the Yankees I was in Haines, Florida, and it was a unique experience. It was my first full experience with segregation. We lived over the tracks, and they paid a guy to bring us every day to the game, to practice. With the Phillies we were in Dade City. It's just an isolated little town. An old Southern town in the middle of Florida.

In 1966 I played with San Diego in the Pacific Coast League for Frank Lucchesi. He was a strange fellow. I couldn't make his team for two years. And then I made it in '66, but I only made it there for about a month. And then I was sent down to Macon. And then I played again for him in '67 and '68, and then again in '69. I don't know how to articulate it, but he was just a strange dude. I don't know if he was hostile toward the Black players, but he certainly wasn't in love with them, that's for sure.

I only lasted twelve games there, initially. What happened was a chain of events. In every organization there was always somebody in front of you. One guy, you know, that you couldn't beat out. And for me in the Phillies organization his name was Bill Sorrell. He was an outfielder and I was an outfielder. Every level that we went to, from AA up, I followed him. So when he was in the big leagues, I went up to San Diego. But when he got sent down to San Diego, that meant I got sent down to Macon.

Macon was the worst experience of my nine years of playing. That was a hell of a place. Oh man, that place was rough. That place was rough. The thing I remember most about it was, about a week before the season was over, we were going to have a barbecue with some of the guys. Two Black guys, two white guys. We went to the park, a state park. We got there

about nine in the morning. So we're getting set up, and all of a sudden these guys come up in this big Buick. I'll never forget it—it was green. And they said to the two white guys with us, "What are these n—— doing here?" And, "Are you n—— lovers?" They saw the barbecue, and said, "No, you're not going to do it here." So we told them . . . we kind of strong-armed them and told them to get on out of there. They said, "We'll be back in a minute." In about fifteen minutes, they came back with about ten cars, full of Ku, Klux, Klans, fully dressed. I said, "Holy shit. We got to get out of here, man." I said, "As soon as this season's over, I'm leaving Macon." The next year the Phillies moved their AA team to Reading, Pennsylvania.

One of the things you have to understand is that, as a player, you went wherever they sent you. And then if you questioned it, you were gone. So if the Phillies would have gone back to Macon, I'd have played in Macon—I'd have played there anyway because you had no choice, especially not being a top Major League prospect. I was not a top Major League prospect. I didn't have enough tools. I was what you'd call a journeyman.

In the Philadelphia organization, and most of the organizations, there were very few marginal Black players. And in Philadelphia, the guys that I played with—and against—Richie Allen, his brother Hank, all those guys, they were guys that had many, many more tools than I did. So I was what's called a marginal player. I didn't know how limited I was as a player until I got to the big leagues and played some big-league games against big-league players. I was very fortunate to have gotten as far as I got.

I was very, very, very surprised when I got called up to the big leagues. I was a pinch hitter in Eugene. I had practically dismissed all aspirations of going to the big leagues, after so many years. And being in spring training in Florida and playing against all of the top players in the world, I knew my abilities were not close to theirs. Because I watched the games and watched them . . . and I knew I couldn't run. So you watch, you watch them hit some balls and then you watch where your balls are going, and you see how limited you are.

I wound up spending a week in the Major Leagues. One week. It was like amazing grace. It was a wonderful experience to play in the big leagues, to warm up with the big guys and to play in the big leagues and to watch some games. And you see where your talent level really is. If I had recognized or understood years earlier what my talent level really was, I'd have left the game a long time ago.

It was amazing that I made it. The only way I can summarize it is that, if there was one thing that most of the players couldn't do, it was out-hustle me. I had one big-league at bat. We had three rainouts. We didn't even go to the park because there was just too much rain. We played one game and then we played an exhibition game against, I think, Detroit. And then the next game, when we came in, Bob Skinner, the manager, called me into the office. He wasn't a nice guy at all for Blacks. Boy, that Skinner. Whoa. He was rough. Straight out of Dixie.

My one at bat was a fiasco. Larry Dierker was pitching and that was the best game he ever pitched in his life. He struck out fourteen that night, and unfortunately, that was my only chance I got to hit. It was a complete blowout. Not even close. You know, people can't see the nervousness in you. But I felt the nerves. I felt completely out of whack. And my best friend was playing second base for Houston at that time—Joe Morgan. I'd known him since we were ten years old. We played Little League together, played together in high school. In fact, I got him into baseball.

When I came back from the Yankees in '62, I was recruited to play for Fitzpatrick Chevrolet. They gave me a utility job—running down parts and stuff, washing cars. And I played for them in their winter semipro league. And they needed a shortstop. So I told them I knew the best shortstop in the world. I told Joe, "Come on out and play with us." And we come to find out that, well, he couldn't make the throw from shortstop. So he switched to second base. And then on that same team they needed a pitcher, so I called my buddy Rudy May. And then the next year they needed a first baseman. So I called Wilver Stargell and he came and played. All for Fitzpatrick Chevrolet. We won a lot of games.

They all became big stars but you know, I never really . . . you never really thought about how they made it and I didn't. You just kept playing and kept hoping. That's all. That's the only thing you can do. You just kept playing.

Anyway, that day, when I came in the clubhouse, I was starting to get dressed and the clubhouse boy told me that Skinner wanted to see me. I went in there and he told me I couldn't hit big-league pitching and he was sending me to Reading. And that was the end of the ball game. After one at bat. I said, you know, he struck out fourteen guys. He struck out Richie Allen four times, Larry Hisle four times; he struck out Johnny Briggs twice. Those guys couldn't hit either. But there was nothing I could do about it. In most cases, when decisions are made, whether you're going up or down or getting cut, the player doesn't have any say-so.

Disappointing is what it was, to go back down. But you know, you went back and tried to play again. But it was a little bit different now because after you watch a couple of big-league games, you realize that you don't have the talent that those guys have. In that exhibition game against Detroit they had Willie Horton and Al Kaline. You look at those guys, you watch Richie Allen hit the ball, and they're hitting it five hundred feet and you're just trying to hit it over second base. So you realize that your talent isn't there. And the speed up there was phenomenal. Getting to the big leagues was an eye-opener. It was a different world.

And then I got traded to Detroit. I got traded for a guy named Monty Richardson. That was a lot different for me because everything was strange to me. Nobody knew me. I had played against some of the guys but by that time my talent was shot. I got a few at bats in Montgomery, Alabama, and then I went to Toledo to play with their triple-A club. I got a few hits but it wasn't enough to stick with the club. My abilities had slipped a lot. I couldn't really run. I mean, I never could run anyway. And now I was even slower. So they released me. I made a couple of attempts to hook on somewhere else but finally I felt it was enough.

I didn't miss baseball when I left it but it was a dream come true. It was fulfilling to be able to go from signing for nothing to go to class-C ball, bounce around, and then finally make it to the big leagues. To go through all the steps that you had to take to get to the big leagues. In order to get to the big leagues you gotta be successful in the Minors. I mean, real successful because there's not a lot of opportunities to fail. If you're pinch-hitting or hitting, you can't go too many games without producing in the Minors. In order to get to the big leagues you gotta produce.

I'm thankful to God that he allowed me to play with all those giants. As I said, if I had recognized, in trying to relate my ability to big-league players while I was in the Minors, I'd have quit a long time ago. You understand what I'm saying? My top speed going down to first base was 4.2 from the left side. That's slow. Guys go down to first base from the left side in 3.9, 3.8. And I had no power. So I was just lucky that I got as far as I did. And I think about that. Watching the guys I played with and guys that I played against, I wonder how I got that far.

6

AARON POINTER

Most of those guys
In their thirties
Had families.
And baseball didn't do anything for them
When they finally
Either
Decided
To
Or were forced
To
Retire.
They left the game with zero.
Nothing.
Not even a thank you.

I grew up in Oakland, California, West Oakland to be precise, and I started playing baseball around eight, nine years old—playing Little League baseball. It's been something I've loved to play my entire life.

My sisters were very successful singers. They're the Pointer Sisters. And we all graduated from McClymonds High School in Oakland, California. I graduated in 1959. There are some other notable athletes that went to McClymonds High School, like Bill Russell, Curt Flood, Vada Pinson, and many others. It was a predominantly African American school but it graduated a lot of successful people, and not only in athletics. Ron Dellums, who was a congressman and the mayor of Oakland, also went there.

After high school I went to the University of San Francisco on a basketball scholarship. I also played baseball at the University of San Francisco, but I got a basketball scholarship because most colleges don't give baseball players full scholarships. They just get partial scholarships. But basketball, I got a full scholarship with room and board, tuition and everything.

I didn't realize—and it didn't affect me—the prejudice and the racism in Oakland, because I was in a neighborhood where people were all pretty much like us. We were poor, but everybody else was poor also. So you really didn't notice the difference. In fact, I didn't know I was really poor until I went to the University of San Francisco. And my roommate had a brand-new Thunderbird. He had money and I didn't have anything except the clothes on my back. For the first time in my life I realized that, hey, I'm poor.

After two years at USF I signed a contract with Houston, mainly to help my parents. They had to move because Oakland was gentrifying—they called it urban renewal—and my parents were forced to sell their house. And so, with my little signing bonus of $10,000, I helped them secure a new home. It was the first time in my life that I had a chance to really help my parents.

At that time Houston was not even officially in the National League. They weren't a club until 1962, but I signed in 1961. That spring I went to spring training in Jacksonville, Florida.

And that was my awakening—when I first saw overt segregation and overt racism.

Although Oakland was not a panacea of liberal ideas, at least in Oakland we never saw "Colored Only" signs over restrooms or water fountains and eating establishments. But in Jacksonville in 1961, when I got off the plane for spring training, it hit me right in the face with those signs: "Colored" waiting room, taxicabs that were for "Coloreds," taxicabs that were for whites. Water fountains that were for "Colored," water fountains that were for whites. The same was true of Salisbury, North Carolina, where they sent me for the season.

And, by the way, in spring training it was really segregated, too. All the African American players stayed in one place and the white players stayed in another place. I can remember the motel where the Black players stayed; it was hot all that time. There were four of us in a room with no air conditioning. We just had fans. It was a miserable place. Amazing that we survived spring training.

Like I said, Salisbury was pretty much the same. I found out right away that there were things I couldn't do. Like going to the parks—you could only go on certain days. I forget what day it was for African Americans at the parks. Couldn't go to the movies because I wasn't welcome. Couldn't go to restaurants because I wasn't welcome. And I was there for five months. It was really miserable. I spent all the time I could around the ball field because that's the only time I wasn't face-to-face with overt racism and prejudice.

Lucky for me, what really helped me make it through that period of time in Salisbury was a historically black college—Livingstone College. I met some people there and they helped me get through the season by showing me where I could go to eat, where I could go to relax on days where the team wasn't playing. During that five-month season I never once had lunch or dinner with my teammates because where they would go for lunch and dinner, I wasn't allowed. Even on road trips to the different cities in the Western Carolina League I couldn't go to the restaurants where they would stop to eat.

I did have one friend on the team, though. His name was Tommy Murray and he would get food for us and bring it back and we would eat together on the bus. Tommy and I were friends, although off the ball field we went our separate ways because where he lived I wasn't allowed to be.

Salisbury was a place that I've never been back to. I've had invitations to go back to Salisbury for different functions, but I refuse to go because there's no reason that I'd want to go back to Salisbury. All of my memories of Salisbury are negative. I had great success on the field that year but I didn't really have any success off the field because of the conditions that prevailed in the South at that time. In fact, I found out years later that in 1961, a freedom-riding group that included John Lewis, the future congressman from Georgia, stopped at Livingstone College on their way to Mississippi for sit-ins. They weren't doing it for voting rights, which Lewis later was deeply involved in, but just for the right to sit at a lunch counter. Later I found out that that bus was bombed by the Klan.

The following year, I went to Oklahoma City. Oklahoma City was Houston's AAA team in 1962—the Oklahoma City 89ers. I played there for half the season. While I was there I shared an apartment with a player on the team who had played in the old Negro leagues. His name was J. C. Hartman. He was an infielder and was very good. J. C. became my mentor. He took care of me. My second year was a lot like the first year because in Oklahoma City segregation was rampant. The places that we had to stay were places that were just not suited for human habitation. But that's what we had to endure.

J. C. played for the Kansas City Monarchs. It was tough on those guys. They had to plan where they were going to stay because they couldn't stay in hotels so they mostly stayed with families that were suggested to them—hey, call this family, they can house three or four of you guys over a weekend, or something like that. I don't know exactly how many years J. C. played in the old Negro leagues but he played quite a few. And he had lived in the South and played in the South with the Monarchs, so he knew what was going on.

J. C. helped to keep me out of trouble because the racism, the segregation, stuff like that, were things that I would have reacted to, you know? But J. C. would say, "Hey, don't worry. This is just the way it is in this part of the country. Don't let it bother you, just do your job and go on with life and just do the best you can. Because this is something you can't change by yourself. So don't let it affect your life." He was a mentor for me in that realm, as far as the socialization, and navigating the kinds of things that Black players experienced in the South in the sixties. He was like a young father figure for me on the baseball field and off the baseball field, keeping me out of trouble and in line as a young, 20-year-old player.

But the coaches could be tough. When I played with Houston in the big leagues—they were the Colt .45s at that time—Harry Craft was the manager. He never said much about anything at all, but having a person like that, who grew up in the South and probably participated, who knows, I can't say one way or another, if he participated in segregation and things that people from the South did at that time, but he and the coaches all were just kind of aloof and I didn't get to know them very well other than on the ball field. We'd go to the ball games. They'd make the lineup, and we'd play the games. After the games were over we'd shower and go home—they'd go their way and I'd go mine. We never saw each other. I never had an opportunity, during the season at any level playing Minor or Major League baseball, to have dinner, lunch, or do anything with the coaches of the teams that I played with. The white players and coaches, they all lived in the same neighborhoods. They could go to the upscale restaurants together. I'm sure the white players had an opportunity to have lunches and dinners and things with the coaches of the teams, because they could go to the restaurants where we couldn't go. All of the towns I played in were segregated—Salisbury, Oklahoma City, Durham, San Antonio. It was pretty much the same in each of those towns.

I don't remember there being any difference in any place that I played. I remember Durham, North Carolina, when

I was sent down from Oklahoma City, the team got me an apartment. It was kind of like a hotel but next to a tobacco-rendering place. Not exactly a rendering place . . . I don't know what you'd call it but it was where they made tobacco. And I can, to this day, smell that smell of the processing of those tobacco leaves.

In 1963 my wife and I had to stay on an air base in San Antonio, Texas, because we couldn't find a place to stay otherwise. That was the only decent housing for us in 1963. In Amarillo, where my daughter was born in 1965, we lived right next to a damn stockyard because the housing conditions were so bad. It was really tough. It's amazing the number of players that were able to keep their sanity playing in the South. I have to admire those guys who stuck it out and were able to continue on playing professional baseball in the South because you were up against it.

Then there was the name-calling from the stands in Salisbury, which happened in other cities, too. You'd hear the N-word damn near every game. It was tough. I was watching TV the other night and I saw an award given to Willie Mays and I can imagine what he went through. Willie played a little bit in the Negro professional leagues. And Henry Aaron, who passed away not too long ago, he played a little bit in the Negro leagues also. I could imagine what they went through in the South and the name-calling and all the stuff that they had to endure in order to just play a game they love. I look back now and I say, Gosh, it's amazing that I was able to make it, to make it through that period of my life and not have it devastate me. Thank goodness for a family that was very supportive, a wife that was very supportive, brothers and sisters who were supportive, and the people I grew up with in Oakland who were very supportive. All of that enabled me to make it through that time because psychologically it was tough.

I would hear those things from the stands and I would just ignore it. If I reacted I probably wouldn't have finished the season. But I just let it go over my head because I couldn't do anything about it. It wouldn't have done any good for me to react. It wouldn't have helped me, it wouldn't help anything. Those people, they want to affect you. They want to make you react. And if you react then they win. And I didn't want to give them that opportunity to affect me and win. So I just ignored it. Didn't say anything back to anybody. Just pretended that I never heard it.

In Salisbury they had sections in the stands where African Americans, people of color, could sit. It was along the first-base line. They couldn't sit anyplace else in the stadium. The other places in the stadium were for whites, although we didn't get that many fans. If you were an African American fan you could only sit along the first-base side in a little roped-off area with a sign that said "Colored Only."

The other places where I played didn't have that kind of situation, as far as a named area where people could sit, but you could see it happening. That's where the white people sit. That's where the people of color sit. You didn't see people of color sitting all over the stadium. They would just be in one place. It wasn't marked, but it was kind of like an unwritten rule. When you buy a ticket to see this ball game, this is where you've got to sit.

But baseball, itself, was always fun to me. My parents and my brothers and sisters used to always tease me, saying that I slept with my baseball glove at night in my bed when I was a youngster growing up. I just loved the game.

You've gotta be lucky in baseball to hit .400. And you know, when you think about hitting .400, you go up to bat ten times and you get four hits. The other six times that you went up to bat, you made an out. So baseball is the only sport that I know of where you go up to bat ten times, get three hits, and you're a star. You play basketball and you take ten shots and you only make three, you're going to end up on the bench. If you play football and you're a wide receiver and you get ten balls thrown at you that you could catch and you only catch three of them, you're not going to play very long.

Baseball is probably the toughest sport to play, but it's more suited to kids that are not physically endowed with being able to jump out of the gym; you don't have to jump out of the gym to play baseball. You don't have to run a 4.3 40 to play baseball. You can be a player like one of my best friends, Joe Morgan. He was like 5 feet 6 inches tall. I don't think a 5-foot-6 player like Joe could have made it in basketball or football, but baseball affords players of all physical sizes and abilities an opportunity to play it.

But as I said, in order to hit .400 you've got to be lucky. Ted Williams hit .400, but I'm sure he was lucky. You've got to get lucky and get a couple of hits when you break your bat, a couple of bloop singles. I was able to run and beat out some infield hits. It's not like you hit a line drive or a double off the wall every hit you get. You've got to get those bloop hits, those broken-bat bloopers over the second baseman's head, hit a ball off your fist and get an infield hit. The key is to be able to put the ball in play. If you can do that then you just have to be lucky. But I also got a lot of legitimate hits. And then there are times where you should've gotten a hit and you didn't. So it all kind of works itself out.

I never paid any attention to what my average was in high school or college. I never even knew what my batting average was. In fact, when I hit .400 in Salisbury, I never really realized the significance of that. Not until 2005 when a reporter from New Orleans called me because there was a player on their

AAA team there, the New Orleans Zephyrs, who was hitting about .390 toward the end of the season. And the reporter asked me if I knew of this player—Rick Short—who had a chance to tie or break my record. And I said, No, I had no idea. I don't keep track of who's hitting what in the Minor Leagues. I just wished him luck. And if he did it, he did it. It wasn't a big deal to me, but it was the first time I realized that hitting .400 even in the Minor Leagues must be significant.

About a week later the reporter called me back and told me that Hurricane Katrina came through New Orleans and wiped out the rest of their home games. He had to play the rest of his season on the road. The New Orleans baseball field was a spacious hitter's ballpark. So he ended up hitting .380 something, having to play the last dozen games on the road.

In 1963 I was called up to Houston near the end of the year. They were the Houston Colt .45s at that time. And at the end of the season, against the Mets, the Colt .45s fielded an all-rookie lineup. It's the only time in Major League history that an all-rookie lineup had played a game in the Major Leagues, I believe. We got beat 10–3. Rusty Staub—he was the first baseman. Joe Morgan was the second baseman. Sonny Jackson, who played a long time with the San Francisco Giants and Atlanta Braves, was the shortstop. A guy by the name of Glenn Vaughn, who got a lot of money to sign, was the third baseman. He only played a couple of years of baseball and just decided it wasn't for him. In left field was a guy by the name of Brock Davis. In center field was Jim Wynn who had a good career with the Houston Astros. The catcher was Jerry Grote. The pitcher was a guy named Jay Dahl. He was a big left-handed pitcher. He was seventeen years old. The next year he was killed in an automobile accident. And in right field was me.

I noticed right off the bat that the talent level at the big-league level was different. Mainly when it came to the pitching. It wasn't the speed—you could see guys that throw just as hard in the Minors, or harder—but that the pitchers had more command, better control of their pitches, and could do a better job of pitching to batters' weaknesses. In the Minors, they didn't keep track of the opposing players, you know, like "This guy likes fastballs, don't throw this guy that." In the Major Leagues it's a science. Every time you came to bat they knew who could hit what.

In the Minor Leagues, you could guess or look for certain pitches at certain times. In the big leagues you couldn't do that. In the big leagues you can't think that because the count is three balls and two strikes you're going to get a fastball because the pitcher doesn't want to walk you. You might get a curveball or a slider, or a changeup, or any pitch. That's the biggest difference.

The living conditions in Houston were better but they still weren't good. The African American community there was a lot larger. There were hotels and motels and apartments where we could stay. My wife and I rented apartments that were good. Whereas in the Minor Leagues, you didn't have that because the community of African Americans in those small Minor League towns was generally small. Houston was a large metropolitan area with a large African American community with facilities that were as good as any facilities that you'd see in any other part of the town.

But it was still segregated. You didn't see the signs that you would see in North Carolina or some of the other places in the South but it was segregated just like Oakland was segregated. You just knew to stay away from this place or that place because the service you would get was going to be terrible. So you could go to a restaurant in Houston in a neighborhood where they didn't want African Americans to eat. And the service would be such that . . . why in the hell would you want to go back to there?

But I feel good about the fact that I had a chance to play professional baseball and I had a chance to play at the highest level of baseball there is on the planet. I reached my goal of playing Major League baseball. I feel really, really good about that. I don't feel good about how I was treated by baseball after I retired; after nine years of professional baseball in the United States and three years in Japan.

Those were the years where, as people would say, you're in the prime of your life. And you spend all that time playing professional baseball, raising your family. And when you retire, you retire with zero. Other than some memories of your experiences playing baseball—a lot of good memories, a lot of bad memories—you're starting your life all over again.

Lucky for me, I had an opportunity in 1970 to play baseball in Japan, and financially, it was the best thing that happened for me and my family because I was compensated probably three or four times more in the three years that I played in Japan than what I made in all nine years that I played professional baseball in the United States. It's too bad that the players in the Minor Leagues are treated the way they are.

I'm not talking about the guys who play one or two years and then they're gone. I'm talking about people that have played in the Minor Leagues for ten, twelve, thirteen years. You know, when I was traded from the Houston organization to the Chicago Cubs organization in 1968, the Cubs sent me to Tacoma. At that time, it was their AAA affiliate. And there were a number of guys there who were in their thirties and had never been to the big leagues. Here these guys are—they're thirty-two, thirty-three years old, playing minor league ball, AAA level—making barely enough to get by. A lot of them by that time had a family. If you were single you could probably get by a little better.

But most of those guys in their thirties had families. And baseball didn't do anything for them when they finally either decided to or were forced to retire. They left the game with zero. Nothing. Not even a thank you. At one point I griped about a little thing that baseball could do. I said at least you can give us some kind of card to let us go to a baseball game for free. Because we can't even get in a game for free.

I just wish that baseball would do better for the players that did so much to make baseball what it is. You look at the financial situation of baseball—a billion-dollar sport—and they can't do anything as far as a minimal amount to help some of the former players that helped promote the game and did so much for the game of baseball. The least they could do is just give these guys something to help make their lives a little better as they get older.

Finally, about five years ago, all of a sudden after complaining and going to the papers, talking about filing a lawsuit against Major League Baseball to have some of our time in the Minor Leagues count toward retirement, and kind of embarrassing baseball a little bit, Major League Baseball started sending players like myself—players who played at least a game in the big leagues prior to 1980—a check. (The Baseball Players Association signed a contract a while back that just went back to 1980—all you had to do is play on a Major League Baseball team for one day after that date and you could get at least a bare-bones pension. If you played before that you got nothing.) I think it was a guilt check or something.

They didn't call it a pension. I remember the first time I saw this—this check from Major League Baseball. I said, What the heck is this for? And they just said, this is a onetime payment. They didn't say what it was for or anything. But it's not a pension, they said. And it's just a onetime thing. After this, there won't be anymore. But then the next year they sent the same thing. And after that I've been getting $1,200 a year from Major League Baseball. I don't know what it's for. It's not a pension. It's not part of their retirement system, but it's something that they decided to give to players that have spent some time playing Major League Baseball before 1980.

Originally there were like eight hundred guys that spent a little time in the Major Leagues that were in the same situation as I'm in who were getting these guilt checks. And it's not just African Americans—there are more white players in that situation than African American players. And now there's like five hundred. And baseball seems to just want to kind of wait us out until we die. It seems like every month I hear of another player who's gone. I'm seventy-nine. To me, it seems like baseball just wants to wait us out until we all die and they don't have to worry about it anymore.

It's a shame that they didn't do more to recognize some of those guys that are in situations that are tough. A lot of guys filed for bankruptcy, have been homeless, have really suffered. They have medical bills that they couldn't pay because they don't have medical insurance. But baseball just seems not to care about those players or what they did for the game or how they contributed to it.

It would have been nice for me just to have a thank you from baseball saying: We appreciate your contribution to the game. Just to let me know that they acknowledge and appreciate what I did as far as promoting and helping to mold the sport of baseball.

7

RON ALLEN

> To finally make the Majors was a feeling of joy
> To finally realize that your dream had come true
> This is what you've been scuffling for
> All the bus rides
> All the balls upside the head
> Drilled in the back
> You did all that to get there
> And all you can say is,
> Oh my goodness gracious.

I signed in 1964 with the Phillies, before they had the draft. To be honest with you, it had boiled down to between three teams. I was playing in a summer league the year before when I got noticed, but it wasn't by the Phillies; it was by the Detroit Tigers. Then, when I was playing American Legion ball one of the Pirates' scouts came to talk to me. Later, I was playing in a summer league tournament and all the scouts were there.

And when the game was over and I went home, there were about three or four scouts stuffed in my mother's living room. And I walked in and she had that look on her face. I was wondering what was going on. And, one by one, they introduced themselves. One was from Cincinnati; one was from Detroit; one was from the White Sox. And one other guy, he was from the Angels. And my mother said to them, "Well, I'll tell you right now, he's not signing with anybody. So, you all might as well just get up and go on home." That kind of threw a monkey wrench into things, you know. I figured, well, maybe by the end of the summer I could talk her into it. But she wouldn't budge. She wanted me to go to college.

The next year I was in the same summer league tournament. One day I hit a home run and everybody was rushing around me, all talking at one time. Joe Lonnett was there and walked up to me and asked me did I ever think about playing pro ball. I knew Joe because he had played with my brother Richie in the Phillies system and he lived literally right down the road from me. So I sat down and talked to him. And I said, "Well, yeah. But I'm in college right now, and I don't know if my mother's gonna let me." So he said, "Well, let me see what I can do." So whoever he talked to, next thing I know, John Ogden was out there. He was the scout for the Phillies that had signed my brother. He had come out to talk to my mother. And then I guess he had come there to try to talk me into staying in college, you know, and not sign. And I kept saying to my mother, "Well, I can always go back to school." Finally, she said to John Ogden, "Well, he's got his mind set on this. What do you think?" Then she said to me, "Do you promise to go back to school?" And I said, "Yeah." She said, "You promise to finish?" I said, "Yes, ma'am." And then Ogden made me promise as well. And that's how I ended up signing. And the next day I was on a plane to Bakersfield, California.

I played both basketball and baseball growing up but wanted to play baseball professionally because one day, when Dick was playing for Little Rock and they came through Buffalo, I went to see him play. Dick Ricketts was pitching and I was talking to him. You know, he was a basketball star around us, in Pittsburgh at Duquesne. And I asked him, "What made you play baseball and not basketball?" And he said, "In basketball there are only gonna be twelve on the team out of everybody in the country. They're only going to keep twelve," he said. The rest all go home. "But here in baseball, you can give yourself five or seven years to make it because of all the teams in the Minor Leagues. And if you don't make it, you move on in life." That stuck with me. And he was right. Because when I got into professional baseball, I saw a whole lot of people there. Yes, indeed. And to be honest with you, a lot of them probably wouldn't have made our American Legion team. And you'd wonder to yourself, "How did he get here?"

I was okay with signing with the same organization that my brothers had signed with because at least I had an idea what the Phillies organization was like. I had gone to see both Dick and Hank when they played in Elmira. And when Dick was in the International League he'd come to Buffalo. And Hank would come to Erie, which was close to us—less than a hundred miles. So we'd go back and forth and I'd be in the locker room and I had an idea of what it was like and I wanted to go. But my brothers was mad at me because they didn't want me to sign. They wanted me to finish college. They was salty because I signed.

I signed in '64 but didn't know too much about what Dick had gone through in Little Rock the previous year because I was in college. He talked about it with my mother so I would come home from college and just catch bits and pieces of what my mother would say about it. You know, about what he had told her about it. I really didn't have much knowledge of how they treated him in Little Rock, what he was going through. Because Dick and I never talked about it. No, we never talked because Dick was kind of a silent person; he kept everything inside. He never displayed that part of it. He just went on about his business. The thing he'd always tell me was, "If you're going to make it, you're going to make it on your own."

I didn't know how professional ball worked and I didn't know that the whole game changes once you signed your name on that contract. And how it no longer becomes a game, it becomes a business. You see, once you sign, the game is no more fun. Little League, Pony League, American Legion ball, you played the game for fun. But when you sign to play professional ball you become a commodity. And everybody that's on your team is striving for the same thing: to get to the big leagues. And the whole game changes around. You become a business. The fun of it is taken out of the game. Because now you're pitted against the twenty-four other guys that's there, you know, trying to get the same thing you want. When you're playing amateur sports, you're just out there because you love to play.

In the beginning, because I had no idea, it was still fun for me. But when you get the gist of what the professional game is about, that changes. And just like being the twenty-fifth man on the team, you're always fighting for a job. And if you're not one of the bonus babies, then you're fighting extra hard for a job.

I'll tell you when it hit me that it was different. It was my second year in Major League camp. And by the end of spring training, you'd see guys just trying to hang on. And you had done your best to get there, and you're fighting for a job just like anybody else. And then they tell you that you can't do this, you can't do that. You did all that to get there, to the Major League camp. But now, the same guys that you hit in the Minor Leagues, all of a sudden they're trying to tell you that you can't hit them because now they're in the Major Leagues.

My first two years I played in the Florida State League.

I remember I had to stay on the bus when we traveled. We couldn't go up to the restaurant and get a meal. You had to wait. Somebody had to bring you a sandwich. I used to get so mad that I couldn't get off the bus at some of the places. And then we stayed over in the Black neighborhood. You know, you didn't stay in the hotel. In '66 I played in Spartanburg in the Western Carolina League and, ooooh, that was an experience. Because, man, you still saw signs of "Colored Only," "White Only," and stuff like that. And there again you couldn't eat here, you couldn't eat there.

When it came to your teammates, you had your closet guys—the guys that would talk behind your back, and then you had good guys. And some of the closet guys you would know—they would know that you had heard them talking, you know. Mostly you learned to deal with it. I went along with a lot of things that I never let bother me. Whatever the way they thought, that was on them. I was here to play.

Some of the coaches was racist from their heart. And it showed. So you just tried to avoid them. A lot of them had come out of that racist mindset—they were still coaching when Jackie Robinson played. I remember I used to ask Hank Bauer what was his thinking back then. And he said he never really thought about it. It was frowned upon. All he said was "That's the way it was." And I thought, Ooooh, man. There were a lot of guys like that. And I was like, My goodness gracious.

At the end of the year in '66 I came up to Tidewater because the Western Carolina League ended earlier. Then I came back to Tidewater the next year and had a real good year. And then it . . . you know, one thing about being a Black kid and having a brother in the Major Leagues, you're always measured by him. And as he was a character, you know, that was tough.

Everybody has ideas in their head. When I played at Reading a couple of years later and we went to Philly to play in the All-Star game there, just 'cause I walked out on the field with the name Allen, man, they booed. Jesus! You know, you wonder what in the world is this all about. They don't measure you by your ability. For me I was measured by my name. And then when you're having a good year, you're always having someone in the organization talking about somebody else. You might be ready for the Major Leagues, but all they could talk about was Greg Luzinski, who was behind me in the system. "Oh, you ought to see this kid that's coming," was all they could say. Well, if he was coming up, great, he's gonna outplay me. If he was better than me he'd have been here and I would have been there, you know. But all you can do is say, Well, look, I'll just keep chugging. One way or another, I'm gonna make it. I ain't gonna let them hold me back.

I do believe that having the Allen name hurt me within the Phillies organization. That's my personal opinion. May not be somebody else's, but that's mine. 'Cause when I was playing in

Reading, I was having a good year, you know, and they needed somebody to call up to fill a spot. You would think I would be the logical person. I don't care if it's one day or two days or what, but they never called me; they called a kid up that couldn't beat me out or else he would've been playing instead of me, you know. And that kinda opened my eyes real good. I don't like running anybody down or thinking I had more talent than anybody else, but I thought I had as much talent as anybody else. But in this game, it's who you know and who likes you, not who's the best man for the position. And a lot of that comes back to the managers and the coaches. Because with some of them, you can tell right off . . . regardless of whether you have a good year, they'll always find something negative to say.

After the 1969 season I was traded to the Mets organization and I was happy to go there. That was one of the best organizations I was in, in professional sports. Whitey Herzog was the farm director then. He was kind of a gruff guy. I just didn't care for him. But as far as treatment went, they were great to me. In that organization it was ballplayer first and everything else second. When I was in the Phillies organization it was just . . . how much money did you get? We got so much invested in this guy but that guy's better than him, but we got this much invested in this guy so he gets sent up. But in the Mets organization, you were just a baseball player. If you had a good year, that's who'd they move up. It didn't make real difference whether you were Ed Kranepool or whoever. If you was doing the job, that's all that mattered.

The Cardinals organization was like that, too. If you was having a good year, they moved you up. I'll say that for them; I'll give them credit for that. And I'll always be thankful for them giving me a shot to get to the big leagues. And it wasn't because I was an Allen; you had to earn your way. It was more about, "Hey, I'm gonna take this kid because he's having a good year." The Phillies were always telling me, "Ah, you stay there, and have a good year." They gave you lip service. That's what I got from the Phillies.

Even though Dick and I didn't speak about what he went through in Little Rock in '63, I came through there when I got traded over to the Mets organization and was at Memphis in 1970 so I got to see it. The Cardinals had a team there at that time, and we went there. It was AA ball, then, and I was just there three or four days or something like that. So I never got to experience all of what he went through. And by the time I had come through there, they had signed the Civil Rights Act or whatever it was Johnson had signed. But when I was there I went to see the school where they integrated, you know. That sort of thing stood out in my mind because I was older and had the benefit of going to college and there were a lot of things I had become aware of. So I was just looking at the history part of it. I wasn't looking at it from the perspective of what Dick went through, his part in all of that. He played for the Travelers, and I think they used to call them the Crackers before that, so I can only imagine.

Although I never experienced what Dick went through, there were signs that were still there. What he had talked about, what he had told my mother, you know. And the people hadn't changed. 'Cause it was just a few years since the desegregation had started. I came through there on the tail end of it. Dick couldn't stay in the same hotels and stuff like that. But we were able to. It was just starting to open up there.

But I tell you, my oldest brother, Coy, made it a point for us to get to see the first-generation guys for ourselves—Jackie Robinson and guys like that. He made sure we got to see them. Guys like Larry Doby, Willie Mays, all of them. He made sure we got to see them. And meet them in person. And when we did, it wasn't like we were awestruck. It was like we knew them and knew what they had been through. I'll tell you one thing though: I wish I knew baseball cards were going to be valuable. Because I would have saved them instead of riding around with them in my spokes. 'Cause all of them Hall of Famers, you know, we were around, and we had their cards. Oh my goodness gracious.

John Ogden was the one who took us down there and introduced us to these guys—Don Newcombe, Roy Campanella—he was in the wheelchair when I met him—Junior Gilliam, who was coaching for the Dodgers. Frank Robinson. All of those guys. You know, you're standing around there with them talking loud, and me, I was just standing there quietly listening.

In '72, when I was with the Cardinals organization, I finally got called up. And I'll tell you: to finally make the Majors was a feeling of joy. To finally realize that your dream had come true. This is what you've been scuffling for. . . . All the bus rides, all the balls upside the head, drilled in the back. You did all that to get there. And all you can say is, Oh my goodness gracious. And then you turn around and look, and you say, Well, I've known these guys ever since I started playing. I felt like I belonged. And that's the only difference between a Major Leaguer and a rookie—knowing that you belong.

In the big leagues, the playing conditions are better. And the competition is better. Like when we used to go in and play the Dodgers, you could get four hard throwers right off the bat. They got the Koufaxes, the Drysdales, and the Suttons, and so on. I had faced Sutton before, when we was in the Florida State League. And when I got to face him at Dodger Stadium, he gave me three curve balls and told me, "Go sit down."

So that's the difference. The better playing conditions and talent-wise, each team may have two or three guys on there that had exceptional talent. And then the other ones were no better than you were. I hit a home run up there. It felt wonderful. You know, it wasn't something that I didn't think I could do. 'Cause I had hit home runs off guys in the Minors that were now in the Majors, you know. So as far as that went, it was nothing new. But, still, I'm in the books!

I was up there for maybe three or four weeks. Got my cup of coffee. And then, at the end of the season they wanted to start bringing up guys from the Minor Leagues. And I probably could have stayed. But at that time, they wanted to take a look at Keith Hernandez. And you could see the writing on the wall. That's what I meant when I was saying that when you learn the game of professional sports, when you've been around awhile, you can see what's coming down the road. It's a business, not a game. And I could see my time was going to be limited there. So I just said, Well, my kids are getting older, and it's time to call it quits.

It was tough to walk away. When the first spring training comes around and you hear that sound of that ball hitting a bat, you say, Oh, man. You can feel the call. And I had thought about going back. But I just didn't want to go through the rigors of the Minor Leagues no more.

I decided to go back to college and get my degree. I had promised my mother and I said, I'm gonna see it through. So I went and got it. And then I worked for the City of Youngstown for a while, for the planning commission. And then I took a job with UPS. I worked there for about ten years. I didn't follow baseball too much at that point. Both Dick and Hank were still playing but I'm telling you, I never went back inside a stadium until my friend, Dusty Baker, got a coaching job and he came to Pittsburgh and wanted me to come down there to see him. And I went down to see him there. And I couldn't get over how small the ballparks had gotten. I said, "Geez, oh man!" The ballparks used to be humongous; when you hit a home run in St. Louis, man, you had to jack that thing. But these looked like a little sandbox. And then when I saw Philadelphia's new ballpark, I thought, "Wow. Man, the ball just jumps out of here."

I don't know why I didn't want to go back to the ballpark. To tell you the truth, I don't know. I don't know why I didn't want to go back. I just didn't have the calling to go back.

Well, I did go back one time. So I take that back. When Dick came to Pittsburgh I went down there to see him. I drove down and then we went in the locker room, saw a lot of guys I had played with. And it was good to see them. But I never had no longing to go back after that.

I don't regret my time in baseball. I had a lot of fun even though I thought I could have been in the big leagues a lot earlier. I am thankful for it because it had shown me a lot. Baseball showed me the country and introduced me to a lot of people that became friends. And I'll be ever so grateful for all of that.

8

ROBERT KELLY

> Certain towns you go to
> You're going to have some people in the stands
> Call you all kinds of names
> You hear them
> You know, people say they don't hear them
> but you hear them
> out there on the field
> You hear them

I signed with the Phillies in, wow, 1965. And I went to spring training in Clearwater, Florida . . . well, it was Dunedin then. And we stayed in a different hotel from the other players. So the Latin players and the Black players stayed in a hotel together. It was kind of out there, away from the regular downtown, you know. I'm from Alabama, so I knew all about the segregation and everything. It was just what you had to go through. The white players stayed in the regular hotel and the bus would come by and pick us up after it picked up the other guys and then they'd drop us off at the complex. So, you know, they only had about maybe thirty Black and Latin players together out of about, what, 250 guys in the Phillies organization?

Judy Johnson was in charge of us and he would tell us different things—what to do and where not to go. And, you know, "Be careful about when you're going out at night." Stuff like that. And he'd tell us about certain restaurants, where we couldn't go to and eat. And just regular stuff that happened at that time down there. There'd be two or three of us sitting down and he would talk to us about stuff like that.

As I said, I'm from Alabama. I went to California as a teenager and I was playing on teams that played the colleges out there. I didn't go to college but we played the college teams. We played them during the week. And on Saturday and Sunday, we would play just organized teams out there.

I knew some guys that played baseball out there. Me and a friend, we went out there and I started playing. . . . Well, I was playing baseball while I was home in Alabama, but we went out there because I knew a guy out there. He played on a baseball team. So we just went out and started playing with them. The team you play with in Alabama is not like the team you're playing with in California. You're going to play with better ballplayers and better conditions and everything. It was an integrated team out there. And some of the guys we played with were playing Minor League ball. Some of them was white, some of them was Black. It's a big difference because, shoot, in Alabama, you're playing on fields that you had to clean off yourself, and then you gotta get all your equipment and everything, you know. So it's a big difference. It's a big deal.

The team I played on was associated with the Phillies. We'd play teams like USC, UCLA, Fullerton, all the teams around there. They had some good players on those teams. We had some pretty good players, too. Some of the guys were playing in the Minor Leagues and some were trying to get signed. We had Enos Cabell, who ended up signing with Houston. And Bobby Tolan. He'd come by and pick me up and then we'd go play the colleges—USC and UCLA. It's hard to remember all the guys. Tolan, he played on Saturdays and Sundays. He had already signed with Pittsburgh or St. Louis, I think, at the time. Brock Davis was there. He played with the Cubs for a while, about three or four years. We were called the Phillies Rookies. That's what we called it.

There were three guys who sort of ran the team: Eddie Malone, Lou Wheatman, and a guy named Nate Dancy. He played in the Negro leagues. They all would get guys together to play the games. Eddie Malone was the guy who signed me to the Phillies. I wasn't drafted. I just signed. They gave me a little money—a thousand dollars, I think.

I played three years in Spartanburg, South Carolina, in the Western Carolina League. And I stayed there three years before I got moved up to another class of baseball, which was in Portsmouth, Virginia. And I played there one year. And then the next year, I went to Reading, Pennsylvania. I played there one year, and I won the batting title in the Eastern League. I think I ended up hitting .323, but it was the highest average.

And then the next year, they moved me to AAA, and I played AAA for about a couple of months, I think. And then they sent me back down to Reading, and I finished the season off there. In '69 I went to the winter instructional league. And I hit .405 or something like that. Pretty much all the players on that team went to the Major Leagues, except me and Mickey Bowers. We was the only two players that was in the instructional league that didn't go to the Major Leagues. I thought I would get invited to spring training since I went to the instructional league and hit good, but they never did invite me.

My manager in Spartanburg was Bob Wellman. I also got to play with him in Reading and in Eugene and he was a pretty nice guy. He never would say anything embarrassing to us but some of the managers I had . . . you know, it's just in the way they present themselves to you. When I played in Spartanburg, my first couple of years, it only was like three, maybe no more than three, Black guys on the whole team. Maybe two. In later years maybe there were a few more Black guys on the team, but no more than three or four. Most of the time it was only two.

It was hard to move up in the Phillies organization. They didn't have too many Black ballplayers in the majors, and I'd play against other farm clubs like Pittsburgh and Houston. Now they had a lot of Black guys throughout their organization, and they would move them up and they'd go to the big leagues. But the Phillies never did move guys up that fast.

The Phillies had a guy, Ronnie Allen. I played AA ball with Ronnie Allen and he was a home run hitter and he hit with a good average. His brother was Richie Allen. They gave him a big-league contract but he never would stay up with the big club. You know, he would go and play with them in spring training and then when the regular season would start he would get sent down to AA, AAA ball. And he was a good hitter. He was a good fielder, but they never would move him up.

We all knew just what he was going through. But, well, you just play and try to do the best you can to stay there and develop yourself. You can't be talking to everybody about it. Because some of the players are probably gonna go back and tell the manager. They didn't ever really tell me why I wasn't moving up and I guess I never did really ask why I wasn't moving up. No one said anything about it. The year that I won the batting title in Reading I thought I played pretty good defense, and I had pretty good speed, but they never did say why I wasn't moving up to the big leagues. They never did say.

When we were in Dunedin, the big-league club trained

in Clearwater and that's when I met Dick Allen. And then in later years we'd train in Clearwater, too, at the complex they had. So we used to see Dick Allen all the time. There was a club we used to go to down there and they would be there—a restaurant—and we would sit down and eat together. It was Dick Allen and Johnny Briggs and Grant Jackson. They all would sit down and talk to us about what we was going through because they had been through the same thing. They would tell us, you know, just be yourself and be careful where you go and try to do everything that you're supposed to do. Do what the people tell you to do because we just didn't have too many Black guys around and we couldn't afford to lose any.

We knew about how Richie was being treated by the Phillies because we would get it from his brother. Ronnie was right there and he was telling us how they treated Richie when he was coming up. They had another brother named Hank Allen, and he was with the Phillies and Washington and the White Sox, I believe. It was hard for him to move up in the Minor Leagues when he was coming up, too. I think he had something like forty home runs one season, and they still didn't bring him up. He did end up playing in the big league, but it took him a long time to make it. So it wasn't just the Phillies; all of baseball was like that. It's hard for you to make it to the big league.

You would see some guys with the Phillies that you thought you was better than they, but they would send them over to play with the Major League club. You know, like some days during spring training some guys go over and play with the Major League club. But I never did get a chance to go over and play with them. And I had had better years than they did in the Minors, but they never would give us, give me, a chance to go over and play with them. I don't know why. It'd bother you, but you can't let that stop you, so you just keep playing and try to do better.

But if you keep playing and they keep sending you back to the same league, you feel like, what do I have to do to get outta here? There's gotta be something. But you see so many guys that come in and then next year they won't be there or they'd have released them, and they don't have no, you know, no jobs. So you just continue to play and try to do better.

You might express your frustrations to your manager or somebody, but you don't want to take it too far because the first thing they'd say is, "Well, you're a troublemaker." You know what I mean? So you try to express yourself, but you don't want to get too overboard with it because you might not be around the next year.

So I would go up and talk to Bob Wellman and I guess I had been around him so long that he knew how I felt about certain things. And I played with Andy Seminick. He never would say that much to you. He was a pretty good guy, but, you know, there's just so many white guys and only a couple of Black guys on the team. You're only going to get so much attention. They mostly gonna lean towards the white guy.

Another manager I had was Nolan Campbell. He was my manager for a while in AA ball. He was kind of a wild guy. He got along with some players, and he didn't get along with other players. I got along with him and I got along with all the managers because I never did give the guys no problems or anything. I just went out and played and tried to do my best.

When we played in Spartanburg, we'd live in a place called the Cleveland Hotel. For the three years that I played there, that's where we stayed. That was about the only hotel in the town, I guess, where we could stay. It was an old hotel, rundown. It was kinda downtown and the restaurants was right around there. So we didn't have to go that far to eat; it was kind of convenient for us. Right across the street, we used to go down to a place and there was a Black lady, she used to cook for us. She had a restaurant, and her name was Ms. Ab. That's where we used to go and eat breakfast all the time. I think her name was Abercrombie, but we called her Ms. Ab. And we used to go down there and she would make us a big breakfast and everything. I had been there so long—for three years—I guess she thought I lived there. It was pretty nice.

There wasn't much mingling between the white and Black players back then, when it came to eating. Most of the time we would go out and eat with the Black guys. In Portsmouth, Virginia, me and Mel Roberts lived with some people in their house. Some Black people. We didn't eat with them, no. We'd always go out to eat. Me and him. But when I got to AAA ball in Eugene, we would go out to eat with some of the white guys. One guy I played with there, his name was John Vukovich. Now, Vukovich was a real nice guy. He would always talk to you when you were on the bus, or when you was going back and forth to the park, or around anywhere.

I think that if I had come along at a different time, I think they would have maybe taken more of a look at me. Or maybe if I was with another organization, they might have taken a better look at me, or something. But with the Phillies . . . I don't know. I played with Andre Thornton. He was very quiet. He later became a minister. We always would go out but we never did go to no bars and nothing like that, because he didn't drink and I didn't drink. We always would go out to eat, you know. See, he was just quiet and he was a good-fielding first baseman. And he had good power. But the Phillies, they weren't hardly gonna give him a shot in the big leagues. He had to go to the Cubs to get there.

I don't know. It's just kinda hard because I played in California and I played against some of the colleges out there. And Paul Owens, he was from California, and he ran the farm system for the Phillies at the time. So he knew how I hit and everything and he always saw me play, but he'd never, I don't know. . . . They just didn't never give me a shot, you know, to play in a higher class of ball.

I did talk to Paul Owens about it and he said, "If I was the manager, I'd take you to the big league as a pinch hitter." But he never did. At that time, Frank Lucchesi was the manager of the Phillies. Frank Lucchesi, he was no good for the Black player. He was a hardheaded guy. And you could tell that there were certain players that he just didn't care for. And then right before that, when Richie Allen was there, he was going his own way, you know, and they just didn't like that. And that's the way it went.

You would think that Paul Owens, who was the farm director at the time, would be able to do more for me. But at that time, the whole Minor League system was just bad. They had guys like Lou Kahn. He was from Georgia. He was a scout and manager in their system, in Eugene and in the Winter Instructional League. They just didn't have nobody to maybe to look over the players better, you know. Because he wasn't right for certain players. Like the Black and the Latin players. He just wasn't right for the job.

You'd hear similar stories from players in different organizations, but you don't want to be talking to everybody because you don't know what the other players will go back and say, you know. So you can't be just telling everybody that "I'm not getting treated right." You might, if you find a guy who you think is your friend, you might talk to him. But you just can't be telling everybody.

I finally gave up baseball after playing a few years in Mexico. I was thirty and it was tough to give it up. But, you know, once you get to a certain age and you see that you're not moving up and you're not making the money that's gonna keep you going, and you've got to come back every year and find a job, it kinda gets up on you, you know?

Looking back on it, what I think about most of the time is that the thing that kind of stopped me was that I wasn't a home run hitter. I remember one scout was telling me that I should try to hit the ball in the air. Because he was telling me when I hit the ball, "You roll your bat over and it causes you to hit a lot of ground balls." Maybe that was one of my problems I should have tried to correct. But at the time, I was just trying to make contact. But now they pay you to try to get it in the air instead of hitting the ball on the ground.

At the time, I thought I was good enough to make it. And I was making good contact with the ball and I always could hit around .300. So I thought that was going to be enough to make it. I started out playing in the infield and then I started to play in the outfield. So not hitting the ball in the air, that could have made a difference.

But I enjoyed myself. I enjoyed it. I enjoyed playing and I enjoyed playing with the guys. I enjoyed a lot of the towns I played in, even though some of the towns wasn't as good as the others. And some of the fans were terrible. When I played in Spartanburg, there was a guy who used to come to the ballpark. He would call me and Roger Nelson all kinds of names. So one day, the general manager and the manager got him up in the office and called us up and asked him why did he come to the park and call us these different names? He said he paid his money; he could do what he wanted to do. Every team that came in, if they had Black players, he would all call them, you know, different names and stuff. He just was a whatever kind of guy, but that's the way it was.

They didn't bar him from the stadium, no, no. At that time, you know, they wasn't gonna do that. They just told him, you

know, you shouldn't do it. This is your hometown team and you shouldn't treat the guys like that. It didn't change anything, though. He kept coming to the games and it was the same old thing. You could hear him all over the ballpark. He'd call you all kinds of names.

Certain towns you go to, you're going to have some people in the stands call you all kinds of names. You hear them. You know, people say they don't hear them, but you hear them, out there on the field. You hear them, what they're saying. But most of the places you go to, the people are nice to you. But you're always going to have one or two people that are just dirty, you know. So you go through all of that. You just shake it off and keep going.

Well, I thank you for taking the time to listen to me. Because I think it's only been once before that somebody asked me about what it was like. Somebody at the paper in Reading,

Pennsylvania, asked me, they wanted to hear how I felt when I was playing baseball. They were pretty nice to me in Reading. They asked me to come back in, I forgot what year it was, 2012, I think, to put me in their hall of fame. They put about two or three more guys in the hall of fame with me that same night. Might have been Robin Roberts and well, I can't recall the other guy's name now. He played with Boston . . . Reggie Smith. And somebody else. I met some people there that night. One of the little boys who was a batboy when I was playing—he was there and he remembered me. That was pretty nice.

9

ROLAND HARDSON

    A lot of ballplayers really got their hearts broken
    Their dreams crushed
    On just stupid stuff
    You're young
    And making
    $500 a month
    During the offseason
    What are you going to do?
    My father died when I was 19
    So
    If it wasn't for my mother
    I'd have been homeless
    Major League Baseball
    Just treats these Minor League players
    Like
        They
        Ain't
        Nothing

When I was just a child, I played other sports better, but I loved baseball much more. I didn't really have to practice or anything like that with football, and I was getting better at basketball, but I just loved baseball better.

My first ten years was in Aliso Village. It's near downtown Los Angeles. And then I moved to South Central Los Angeles. I had some good times. You know, when you're young, you don't think about a lot of things, but it was a rough area to grow up in. I got stabbed three times when I was ten years old—twice in my back, and once in my face, right at the top of my head. I knew the one person that stabbed me on top of my head, but the other two I didn't. It was just a rough neighborhood. You had to learn how to fight to survive. I don't really even remember the circumstances around any of that. 'Cause you know, I was young. I'm seventy right now. I just didn't think about it afterwards. Being a young kid, you don't think about things like that. I did have to go to the hospital all three times. I got stitches. The one on top of my head, I can't see that no more. But the ones in the back—you might be able to see one of them, but the other one, I think, is probably gone. I really can't see my back. I don't look at it, really. And I don't think about it at all.

When we moved to South Central, it was rough but not as rough as Aliso Village. But that was when I really started playing hardball. Down at Aliso Village, we used to play softball, basketball, football, track, and things like that. And then when I moved to South Central, I started playing hardball. Do you remember Dan Ford? He used to play with the California Angels. He and I and a few other guys all grew up in South Central together and we all used to walk from Fifty-Sixth and Central all the way to South Park, which is Fifty-First and Avalon in Los Angeles. We walked, I guess, about a couple of miles to the park to play hardball.

There was a league, there. An organized little league. The little league had kids that ranged from twelve and under.

And then you had a junior league that went from thirteen to fifteen. And then you had a senior league that started from sixteen and up. You remember George Hendrick? He played in front of me. When I was in the little league, he was in the senior league. And sometimes the senior league would play games in Wrigley Field—the stadium the Angels played in when they first started in Los Angeles. It was a big stadium. A huge stadium. And he would hit home runs into the seats there. At sixteen years old.

But Dan Ford and me, we grew up together and used to practice all the time. We played in the streets and in this guy named Dwayne Tagger's driveway, and we had to quit playing in the streets 'cause we busted out too many windows. We would use a rubber ball—a hard rubber ball—and we busted out so many windows we had to go to the tennis balls. Our parents didn't like it too much, us doing all that. Because they had to pay for the windows.

And then I got separated from Dan Ford and Dwayne. They went to Fremont High and I went to Jeff—Thomas Jefferson—in Los Angeles. The dividing line was one street north of our street. But because Dan Ford and Dwayne Tagger's parents had gone to Fremont themselves, they got permission to go there also. How they did it, I don't know. Some say they used different addresses.

I wanted to go to Fremont, too, because that's where the top ballplayers went: Willie Crawford, I think Bobby Tolan went there too. They had nothing but top athletes come out of there: George Hendrick, Chet Lemon, Bob Watson. And the coach was Mr. Phil Pope, who had a connection to the Oakland A's. He would inform the club of certain ballplayers that he had. He was a very, very, very nice man. He treated us with respect. He and a scout for the Pirates named Dick Cole were the only scouts who would come into the South Central

area. The other scouts, they would come, but they would dart in and dart out real quick. They stayed no more than a half hour to an hour, at the most. And then they were out of the neighborhood. They wasn't interested in us city kids.

When I graduated out of high school, I played at Ross Snyder Park, under Chet Brewer, the old Negro-league baseball player. He used to be a pitcher. And he used to tell us stories about the old Negro leagues and how they traveled and stuff like that. He told me that he pitched for the Kansas City Monarchs, and some other teams. He said they would travel in cars—station wagons—pile everybody up and go city-to-city on the East Coast and the Midwest, California, Mexico. He said that they would be shut down near every time they'd go to a ballpark. They were getting interfered with quite a bit by the officials of the towns.

They would also travel in buses and sleep in the luggage racks above the seats. They had it pretty hard because a lot of places they stayed, when they were in the United States, they had to go in the back of the hotels, and a lot of hotels wouldn't allow them to stay there at all. So they slept on the bus or when it was kind of nice out, they slept right outside the bus, on the ground.

Listening to all of this, it was kind of weird. You know, they tell you these things but you really don't know about it. Well, when I went to Prairie View A&M, and when I played in the Oakland A's organization, I experienced it, what they were saying. You know, we used to travel in those buses too, in the Minor Leagues. And on the long rides from Lewiston, Idaho, to Canada or Bellingham, Washington, or Walla Walla, we would sleep up there, too. Quite a few of us used to sleep up there with the luggage. Also, some of the hotels didn't allow us to stay there. So we had to find a hotel that would accommodate Blacks. And some of the stores we stopped at on the way . . . I went in the front door one place and the guy that was behind the counter—a Caucasian guy—called me the N-word. And I kind of looked around, like, who was he talking to? And he told me it was me. He told me, Why did I come through the front door? I got upset, and I told him I would whoop his ass if he kept calling me that name. And he told me, Yeah, he'll shoot me dead, too. And my teammates, they all tackled me down, and took me out of the store and said, "You were supposed to go around." And I said, "Well, I didn't see nothing." One guy said, "There's a big old sign right above your head." The racism was right in your face. I wasn't used to that.

I ended up signing with the Oakland A's organization and was sent to play on their rookie league club in Lewiston, Idaho. I didn't like the way they did things, because of a guy named Buddy Peterson—you remember that name. He was the manager of my rookie league club: the Lewiston Broncs. He didn't say much to us, but he called me and a couple of other Black ballplayers into his office one time and he told us, "Don't mess with the snow." So we tell him, "Well, we ain't on no drugs. We don't mess with that stuff." He said, "That's not what I'm talking about. You know what I'm talking about." He meant that if we got caught messing with white girls or white women, we were going to get released from the organization.

Buddy Peterson had no interest in any Black ballplayer. Matter of fact, he didn't say too much to us. He would just walk around in a daze with his arm out, like he had this little imaginary dog he had on a leash. We stayed away from him as much as we could, especially after he told us that. Because we had some neighbors in the place that we rented. They were two young white girls who had an automobile. And they would give us a ride to the park. And we would give them passes to see the game free if they wanted to. And sometimes they left, but they always came back and picked us up to take us home. And Buddy Peterson got a whiff of that. So what we did, we snuck rides with them to the ballpark, and they would drop us off, maybe a block or two away from the ballpark, and then we walked the rest of the way to the stadium, just to keep Buddy Peterson from seeing us.

We found that in a lot of cities you didn't see too many people of color coming to the ballpark. We would see them when we were in Portland or Seattle. But when we went to Bellingham, Washington, or to Westminster, Canada, we, or at least I, didn't see very many Black people at all. Places like

Tri-City, maybe one or two Black people used to come to the ballpark there.

When we would go to Portland, the fans would throw sodas on us. One guy had soda in his mouth and he spit on me. And I took a couple of baseballs, and before I got a chance to throw one at him, my manager grabbed me. And then Tom Trebelhorn and a couple of ballplayers said, "Nah, don't do that. Don't do that. We'll get in trouble." I said, "Well, look at my uniform. He spit all this soda on it, you know." We'd be on deck and people would throw rocks at us or say nasty things to us. Just all kinds of nasty things.

You know . . . I just don't . . . It's in the past. Ain't nothing gonna be done about it. But it was just terrible. It makes you feel like you don't want to be there, or they don't want you there. That's how you feel. So, of course, you can see the results of it now. The inner-city Blacks won't play baseball. They won't play it at all. We were told that we had to be twice as good—or more—as our Caucasian friends in order to make it. That's why we play so hard. Otherwise, we don't get the same opportunity they get.

The only two coaches that showed interest in the Black players were two coaches I had in spring training: Tom Trebelhorn and Rene Lachemann. And just about all of the players. They knew how difficult it was and they tried to make it pleasant for us. And it kept our minds off of it, in a way. I was called to Lachemann's room during spring training. He cooked for everybody who he said was going to start for him, who he was taking to the California League with him. Of course, I never got there because they released me.

I'll tell you two incidents. One time, I went out in the outfield during spring training after my year in the rookie league, and someone hit a high fly ball. I lost it in the sun and the ball hit me in the chest. And I said, "I lost it in the sun." But John Claiborne, the farm director, was asking me how come I ain't wearing sunglasses? I said, "Well, the sunglasses that you guys give us are all scratched up." He said, "You could have bought your own." And I said, "Yeah, if you guys would pay me a salary."

They gave me $500 a month. And then my next year, they gave me $675, which is no money at all. Meanwhile, these other guys, these white guys, were driving up in brand-new cars because their paychecks were huge because they got signing bonus money along with the $500.

Anyway, I got in a hassle with John Claiborne for not wearing the glasses, my sunglasses. Then he yelled at me again. Wayne Gross hit a ball to the fence, and I let it go over for a home run. I could've caught it, but I let it go for a home run because I'd have had to jump up in the air to catch it, but they had a chain-link fence there and it had those crisscross points. And I didn't want to land on top of that. So I said, This is just spring training. I'm gonna just let it go. So I let it go. When I came in, he started yelling at me and, I don't know, I guess I had just had enough of the BS. Because I knew it was BS. I just told John Claiborne if he yelled at me again, he was going to be picking himself up off the ground. I was going to knock his old ass out. He best not yell at me no more.

So the last day of spring training, when we were getting ready to depart, to go to our respective stadiums, he released me. And I said, well, okay, that's cool. I didn't have the desire to play pro ball anymore because anybody could come along and figure that they could talk to you any kind of way they want. They can treat you the way they want and you've just got to sit there and take it. Well, I wasn't gonna take it. Growing up in South Central LA, going into the white community, dealing with them calling me racial names. Being a Black person it's almost like an everyday occurrence—the white folks picking at you all the time like you don't belong. So I didn't want to play ball anymore. If I had to do what Jackie Robinson had to do, I wouldn't do it. I'd probably be dead or in jail for kicking somebody's behind because I wouldn't take that stuff. I just had enough of that.

I'll say this to you before I forget, and hopefully you'll remember this: I came up as a catcher and Chet Brewer started me behind the plate. I caught Doc Ellis, Larry Demery, Randy Johnson when he was at USC. Matt Young, Bert Blyleven. But when I played professional baseball, the Major Leagues, and the Minor Leagues didn't give Blacks the opportunity to become catchers. Now, I know you would probably say, well, John Roseboro, Manny Sanguillen, and other guys like that were Black and were catchers. But what I'm talking about is that there weren't enough guys to fill one hand. And there were some really good catchers coming out of Southern California.

There never were, and still aren't, a lot of Black catchers. There were always a few but most of the time they'd move you to a different position. Gary Alexander, Pedro Guerrero: they were catchers in the Minor Leagues. But they moved them. At that time, it was almost like the quarterback position in football. They're supposed to be the guys that control the game—the leaders. And they didn't want that. Now, I know, people may say, well, you just saying that just to say that. But I'm really not saying that just to say that. Gary Alexander was an excellent catcher. Pedro Guerrero was too. And why, when they got to the big club, why weren't they at catcher? Now, Gary caught every now and then in the Major Leagues, but they would often put him on first base or third base or DH him. And me, they moved me to the outfield. I'd see some of the guys I used to play with and they would ask me, "How come you're not catching for the Oakland A's?" I'd say, "Well, they signed me as a catcher, but they put me in the outfield, and they told me I won't be catching." I'd tell them there was nothing I could do about it. You know, I signed the contract because I wanted to play pro ball. But once I did . . . Al Downing, remember him? He gave up Hank Aaron's 715th home run. Al Downing was a helluva nice guy. He'd seen me play. And he told me, "I can't understand why you don't get a chance." Bobby Castillo—he had the best control of any pitcher I ever caught—used to tell me that I should be in the Major Leagues, catching. I'd say, "Well, they won't let me catch."

The competition in the Oakland organization was stiff. They still had Claudell Washington, Reggie Jackson, and all. They had George Hendrick, Joe Rudy, Sal Bando, Phil Garner. So nobody's really moving up within the organization except the pitchers. And, as far as Black catchers, that wasn't happening. And we kind of knew it. It's sad that they treat ballplayers in the Minors like that. They just don't have respect for you. The guys are working their hardest, doing their best. I used to go to the batting cage owned by Babe Dahlgren, and I used to hit so long there that my hands were bleeding. You ever hear of a guy named Babe Dahlgren? He replaced Lou Gehrig at first base. He had a batting cage out in Arcadia—it was an old bowling alley. He improved my hitting, helped me to get my timing. Taught me to move my hands before the ball was thrown. I was hitting the ball so hard I thought I was hitting the cover off the ball. We used to sit down and have long talks with him. And he used to tell us about the Major Leagues quite a bit. He told us that just a small amount of people are gonna be able to make it in. So regardless of how good you are, if your position is the same as a superstar's, they're not going to look to bring you up. If you play the same position Reggie Jackson played, don't even think about coming up. Because you're not. And if you're behind Lou Gehrig, forget it.

After I was out of baseball, I caught quite a few of the Major League ballplayers during the winter. They needed people to work out with them at Brookside Park, needed somebody to throw the ball to. I was a catcher and I had some equipment. So they'd pitch, they'd get their throwing in. And then when spring training came around, they'd be ready to go. There were three of us who would catch them. Me, Gary Alexander, and another guy whose name I can't remember who was also a helluva ballplayer. He had signed with Baltimore as a catcher and they released him, too. Every once in a while we'd sit down and Gary would tell us that the Major Leagues just doesn't want Black guys as catchers so we had to learn another position. Baseball may deny it, but that's cool. I couldn't care less what they do now. If they were about to go over a cliff, I wouldn't try to stop them.

I like the game of baseball. I liked the traveling and playing in the different cities. But I didn't like a lot of the other stuff. When we traveled on the road, they used to give us five dollars a day for meal money. And I used to eat. I didn't joke around. And five dollars wouldn't get you much. So we'd try to find smorgasbords, like Sir George's, or whatever they used to call them. Anyway, they had to kick us out of there. If we had a night game, we would wake up early and if we didn't have practice, we'd go into these towns for smorgasbords to make our money last. We'd try to sneak food out of the smorgasbord because you gotta eat everything there. You can't take anything out, but we would sneak some food out so we could have it to eat later.

After I got released by the A's a man named Spider Jorgensen offered me a contract with the Cincinnati Reds. And, I told him "I don't want to play professional baseball anymore. I don't even want to play baseball for a living at all." 'Cause during the offseason, we wasn't getting paid, so I was unemployed. And when I went to the unemployment office, they told me I couldn't get it. So I didn't get that. I had to go back and rely on staying with my mother. You know, my mother—she had eleven kids; it was eleven of us. I didn't want to put no more burden on her. So I just went on and got me a job at a UPS. See, I'd just had a child and I had to pay child support. And the money I was making playing baseball wasn't enough to live on and pay child support. So I had to get out and work. Also, in baseball, you get hurt, what medical do you have? We never knew. I mean, I got hit many times in the Minor Leagues and never went to a doctor, never did nothing. When I started working steadily, then I realized that my salary was paying for my medical and stuff like that. I get sick, I can go to the hospital. I got a doctor's card, where I could pay my payments or they'll pay it for me. In baseball, we had nothing like that. The sad thing about it is, you'd think you're doing pretty well, right? And then all of a sudden they release you. Well, you know something, a lot of times guys just bought houses or just started a family, and then got released. It kind of breaks your heart. They try their best to get back in, but you gotta have a salary to pay your bills so you can live. And they just leave you out in the cold, just like that.

A lot of ballplayers really got their hearts broken, their dreams crushed, on just stupid stuff. You're young and making $500 a month; during the offseason, what are you going to do? My father died when I was nineteen so if it wasn't for my mother I'd have been homeless. Major League Baseball just treats these Minor League players like they ain't nothing. There should be something they could do. Maybe not pay a salary all year round but give a guy a course or something to help him get through the offseason—what can he do until the season reopens? What kind of part-time jobs could you get so that when the season ends you can go to work? They just leave you out in the cold. They could care less. All they want to do, if they can make money on you, they'll make it. If they can't, they get rid of you, and go find somebody who they can.

I met a lot of great guys in baseball. Like Bobby Castillo. I loved Bobby Castillo. He was an All-American high school ballplayer at Lincoln High. The Royals drafted him in high school. He played a year in their system and then got released. The same year I got released. So we both came home and said, wow, this is a coincidence. And we both decided to try our luck down in Mexico. And I came back within a week. I said, "I can't do it. I can't speak the language. And I can't eat this food." I couldn't stop crapping. And I said, "I got to go home, man. This, this stuff ain't mixing with me." But he stayed and played for a team near Tijuana. Anyway, he pitched and he ran into Fernando Valenzuela. See, Bobby Castillo told me that he was the one who taught Fernando how to throw a screwball. Because Bobby's screwball was almost like a left-hander's curve. It didn't have that real hard break, but it broke like a curve, like a left-hander throwing a curve.

After I left baseball I watched it quite a bit because some of my friends were playing. And then as the years went by, I started watching less and less, usually just the playoffs and the championship. And now I'm at the point where I just watch mainly the championship games. But I won't watch too much. I was watching the California Angels the other day, and I got so bored listening to the analysis that I started watching women's softball. Then I got bored listening to that. They think that the ballplayers, or pitchers, or whoever, could have done this, should have done that. Analyzing everything. But it's different when you're out there on the field playing. Because anything can happen. That analysis can't explain everything. Like once, when I was playing in Lewiston a pitcher came in to relieve. And I was the first batter who was going to face him.

And a bug flew in my eye. I couldn't get it out. The trainer was trying to get it out, and nobody could get it out. So they had to have another batter bat for me. That pitcher was a friend of mine. I see him every now and then and he teases me about it today. He tells me, "Yeah, you just didn't wanna face me." And I say, "Yeah, you're probably right. That was cool. I didn't want to face you anyway."

10

JOHN THOMPSON

> It wasn't a big bonus contract.
> I got some money,
> A glove,
> And they bought me shoes.

I played from '69 to '71. And you know, I had good managers—my first two years. I didn't get drafted out of high school, which really shocked and surprised me because I was all this and all that, all-league and first-team, through my junior and senior years at Compton High School. I was very productive there. And I was disappointed because at the time they had twenty teams in the Major Leagues, and I filled out scout cards from sixteen of the twenty clubs. Sixteen—that's pretty good; you figure you're going to get drafted. And I happened to graduate in 1965, which was the year they started the draft. When I was a junior, I hit .527, which was unreal. And I was a switch-hitter. I hit both left- and right handed with power. And I ran to first base in 3.3 seconds; that's pretty fast. In my senior year I tailed off to .327 but I still made first-team all league.

I loved the sport. Mickey Mantle was my favorite player. Vin Scully said that Willie Mays was the best player he ever saw and I kind of agree with that, but Mickey Mantle was the one I idolized because he was a switch-hitter.

I also played with a team called the Pittsburgh Pirate Rookies, which was mostly all Black, for a guy named Chet Brewer. He was a pitcher in the Negro leagues. I played with a lot of good players—George Hendrick was in left and batted fifth. Leon Murray, who was Eddie Murray's brother, played first base and hit cleanup. I hit third in the lineup.

A strange thing happened. I don't know if you ever heard of Jerry Gardner, but he was a big-time scout with the Pittsburgh Pirates back in the day. One day he was there when I went four for five and threw out two base runners. And Chet Brewer said, "Look, John, after the game we're going to come by your house. You don't need an agent or anything. You name your price." That's how good I was hitting with the Pirate Rookies. My mom had actually repainted the living room with my neighbor, so the house could look nice. But they never showed up.

And that hurt my heart. I kept playing for him, Chet Brewer, but I was very disappointed in him because he didn't even tell me why they weren't coming to my house, never called me. But I played out the schedule; the next game I was there. But then I met a man named Robert Pierce, who, after I hit a couple of home runs in a game, said, "I'm gonna have a team in '68. Tommy Davis, Sandy Koufax, and Don Drysdale's gonna sponsor it." Sure enough, they did, and I joined him.

That's how it started for me, until I signed in '69. Bob Pierce's team was called the Compton Browns. He managed the team. He was an actor, too; he went by Stack Pierce. Tommy Davis was a two-time Major League batting champion. And like I said, there was also Sandy Koufax and Don Drysdale. I knew all of them, personally, met 'em. I sat right next to Sandy Koufax, when I first met him. It was just a great experience.

I forget the organization Pierce played with, but he didn't make the Majors. Both Tommy and Pierce knew Lou Dials. Now you may not have heard that name, but he played in the Negro leagues way back when. Later he was a scout with the Kansas City Royals. He was a very nice guy. He came to scout me one game, and I think I went 4 for 5 with two homers, a double, and a triple. And I guess that caught his eye and got his interest because he called me a few days later and said, "Hey, we'd like to sign you."

Then Lou Dials brought a guy named John "Spider" Jorgensen to see me play. This was in the city of Compton, at a stadium called Cressey Park. Cressey Park, at that time, was a hot spot for scouts to come see players.

So Spider came to see me with Lou Dials. And I went 3 for 5 in that game, and the first one hit right off the wall, right center field. Spider Jorgensen really liked that. He talked to me after the game and he says, "I think you'll be a fit; it'll be a good opportunity for you to come play for me in Winnipeg, Manitoba."

And I said, "Yeah, I'd love to do that." I was excited. A couple of days later they called and said, "We want to sign you." So we went to where Rosie Gilhausen lived. I think it was in Fullerton; he had a really nice home. I don't know if you've heard of Rosie Gilhausen, but he was a scout for the Angels, a big-time scout. And then he moved over to the Kansas City Royals organization when they started up in 1969. And that's where I signed—with the Kansas City Royals in 1969. It wasn't a big bonus contract. I got some money, a glove, and they bought me shoes.

My first year was in Winnipeg, Manitoba—low A ball—playing for Spider Jorgensen. He played with the Dodgers and I have a picture of him with Jackie Robinson, who he played with in '47. It was a great shot. He never talked about it. He

never brought it up. On the field I didn't hit well—I hit .136. I had 103 at bats that season, but only fourteen hits, three homers, and fourteen RBIs. But I will say that my first hit in professional baseball, after going 0 for 7 in a couple of games, was a grand slam home run. In a game we won 11–7. I was thrilled about that. Still have the baseball, as a matter of fact.

It was great, living in Winnipeg. We had the largest city in the league. And the people were just the greatest. I still have friends there that I met way back when in '69. It was just fantastic. They would actually open up their homes for you if you didn't have a place to stay and stuff like that, and they hardly even knew us. The city had a half a million people. You go to these other small towns, you might have twenty-five thousand. So all the teams in our league looked forward to coming to Winnipeg. We had games shown on TV. Not every day. But on most weekends.

I was among the first arrivals that year and the first arrivals initially stayed in a hotel near Polo Park. There was a good-sized mall and a couple of hotels around there and that's where most of the players stayed when we first arrived, for about a week or two. Eventually I found a nice small hotel and then, I don't know if I'd call it a major hotel, but they had enough rooms and I was able to get one. It was very reasonable considering that we got around $500 a month.

As I recall, we had three Black guys on the team: myself, a guy named Art Demery, whose brother, Larry Demery, played for the Pittsburgh Pirates, and Dave Thornton. So we had three Black ballplayers out of a roster of maybe thirty-plus players. Most of us were kids. A lot came out of college, though. Some were drafted but we also had players who were free agents.

I was one of them. I was not drafted, like I said. I don't know why. At the tryout camps, people said I did great. Anyway, our season was what was called a short season because a lot of players there were coming out of college and they didn't get out of school until May or June. So we started in June, officially, but I signed in March. So I had six to eight weeks to prepare myself—exercise, go to the batting cage and stuff like that, prior to actually going to Winnipeg.

Spider Jorgensen and my coaches were great. We didn't have a pitching coach. I don't know if it was finances or whether it was something like, you know, how many guys can we send to work with these fellows. In my second and third years they had more people to work with you personally. Joe "Flash" Gordon, a Hall of Famer with the New York Yankees, and Tommy Henrich—he played alongside Babe Ruth and Joe DiMaggio—worked with us. Henrich played right field. Heck of a guy. That's when I really began to hit the ball.

I might've said I was a switch-hitter, which I was. But Spider only allowed me to bat right-handed. I said, "Spider, I hit left-handed too." He said, "Yeah, but when I saw you, you were hitting right-handed, and we signed you as a right-handed batter." But that was only because I was facing a left-handed pitcher when Spider saw me. So he thought I was just a right-handed batter. And on my contract, I told Rosie Gilhausen when I signed at his house that I was a switch-hitter, and he put that down. So that's the way it was written up. But Spider would never let me switch-hit. And it really bothered me because, obviously, you see more right-handers than lefties in baseball.

And I hit better left-handed even though I was a natural right-handed hitter. I think that, really, that's why I struggled. I had to learn how to hit all over again, just from the right side. In fact, I don't think, I know it hurt me. And that's reflected in my stats that first year—a .136 average.

As for how that happened, well, here was a guy—Spider Jorgensen—who was talking to me after I waited for years to sign a baseball contract. And he saw me hit left-handed against a left-handed pitcher during batting practice one day and he asked me why was I hitting left-handed? You know how you just go switch from left to right and back to take some pitches during batting practice? So I said, "Well, because I'm a switch-hitter." And that's when he told me, "We signed you as a right-handed batter and you're gonna bat right-handed." End of story.

So here I am, having waited for years to sign this contract and play baseball and get that opportunity. I wasn't going to argue with him. I wasn't going to say, "Hey, I've been doing this since Little League." So I said, "Okay." I didn't want to get released the first season because there was a misunderstanding over whether I could bat both left and right.

Waterloo—my second year—was when I had my best year. I started slow. I started 2 for 18. My manager was Steve Boros. He played third base with the Detroit Tigers back in the day. He played with Al Kaline. He was my favorite. I had a hamstring injury coming out of spring training that year and they sent me to Mesa, Arizona. When you get injured and you're not ready to really join a team, just like in the Major Leagues, they send you to places like Mesa, Arizona.

And so I went to Mesa and we played against other guys who had either been injured or who were getting a late start in spring training. That's when I met Joe Gordon. He worked with me. I mean, he really worked with me. So did Tommy Henrich.

When I got to Waterloo, like I said, I started slow. But after I went 2 for 18, I just went on a tear and really started stroking the ball. One time, I think in the middle of the season, I was hitting about .383. I was leading the league in hitting for a month. I ended up only hitting .261. I don't know what happened, I just went in a terrible slump. I was still batting right-handed and I didn't even ask Steve Boros . . . he never knew I could hit left-handed. I just wanted to be a good guy. And I think that really hurt me.

One time I hit four consecutive home runs. My last at bat one night I hit a home run and then the very next day I hit three consecutive home runs off Bill Travers. He played in the Major Leagues. He was a tall white kid, about 6 foot 4. Threw nothing but heat. I mean heat, heat, heat. And I was a dead fastball hitter. There were some writers there in the local Waterloo papers who thought that I had at least tied a record or something. And they found out that five consecutive home runs was the record; hit by Dick Stuart, who ended up playing for the Pirates. He probably still has the record. But I hit four so I was proud of that. I've got one of the baseballs— the third home run ball. You know, the kids find them and you give them a couple of bucks. So I have that ball.

One time we're playing Quincy, which was a Cubs farm team, and Bill North was in the batting cage before the game. They had just sent him down from AA and our pitcher, Doug

Bird, was listening because he was going to pitch that night and he's got to get his swings in too because they didn't have a DH then. Doug Bird ended up pitching for the Royals in the Majors. The Royals, Yankees, Chicago Cubs. Great guy. Anyway, Bill North was hitting and he says, "You know, I don't know why I'm down here with you guys." We all heard it, because we had players getting ready to go in the cage after he hit. He says, "I don't know why I'm down here with you guys. You guys really aren't in my league. You're down here for a reason in A ball. And I should be in the Major Leagues." And he's popping off. First pitch of the game, Doug—who had great control—hit him right in the head. You just don't say that kind of stuff. He was demeaning us. First pitch, he went down like somebody shot him. Knocked him out of the game; he was gone.

As for where I lived in Waterloo, it was still the Minor Leagues, so we're not getting a lot of money. I can't remember if we went up in salary at all; we might've gone up a hundred bucks over the $500 I made the first year. They weren't going to give us some elaborate amount of money, double it or something like that. Nobody got that. Four of us ended up renting a house close to the ballpark. We could walk to it. It was maybe a half mile from it. It was me, John "Sunny" Dixon, an African American pitcher from Sacramento, Joe Nunn—a pitcher from Birmingham, Alabama, and Doug Bird. Doug Bird was my favorite guy. He was from Corona, California. There was enough room for all of us in that house so it was nice.

But Waterloo wasn't like Winnipeg, where you had places to eat. You were lucky to find a greasy spoon or something like that. After a game there weren't many options; the whole town just shut down. One thing I did see a lot of were John Deere tractors. Everywhere you would look it was John Deere, John Deere, John Deere. And the guys would say, "If we don't make it we might have to live here. We're gonna have to stay here and we'll drive tractors or sell them." We all got a kick out of that because that's all we saw. It was hilarious. There was no city life, no clubs. In Winnipeg you could find a place to go dancing and stuff like that. Good music so you could kick back after a game. But Waterloo? No. It was strictly business.

But there wasn't any sort of segregation there. Not at all. And I'm going to tell you a story. I don't think I've told this to many people. We were coming out of a Shakey's Pizza in Cedar Falls, some buddies and I. We were going to see the movie *Patton*, with George C. Scott. So we're leaving and these two white girls were coming in. They were students at the University of Northern Iowa, which is in Cedar Falls. And I'm holding the door open for them to come in. And one of the girls says—and I'm not going to say the word but she actually did say it—"I want to f*** you." And I said, "What? I'm sorry, ma'am. What are you talking about? I don't know you, you're not my girlfriend, yada, yada, yada." And then she repeated it. And I said, "Oh, my God." My buddies were looking at me like, John, what are you going to do, man?

She was a gorgeous girl. She had Shirley Temple hair, but black, not brown like Shirley Temple had it. But she was dropdead gorgeous. And I thought about it. But I didn't know these towns and I didn't know these people and I didn't know what she was getting at. I had enough proof to say, "Hey, it was consensual, because there were four of us there who heard this." But I didn't do anything. I just said, "Well, my pleasure meeting you but we've got to get to a movie." And I walked away.

She said she lived in Mason City, Iowa. I had to look it up afterwards to see if she was just . . . was this a gimmick? A trick? What? If you're African American you've just got to be careful. I grew up in Compton. I had never been out of Compton except to go to Winnipeg my first year. But that shocked me. I didn't expect that. When I was closing the door for her as she was going in, she says, "You sure you don't want me to follow you?" And I said, "No, I don't want you to follow me." I tried to be nice, but I couldn't do that stuff. She was well-dressed, well-groomed. I don't know where that came from. I don't know any of that stuff. I didn't ask those kinds of questions. I just went about my business, kept my nose clean. As my mom said, "Be careful out there."

As I said, Steve Boros was my manager that year and he was the greatest guy I think I've ever met in baseball, in terms of my three seasons. All the players loved him. And here again we didn't have any assistant coaches. We put a player on first base to be the first-base coach; we had a trainer who drove the bus.

One time we were playing in Wisconsin Rapids. I think they were the Milwaukee Brewers farm team. And a lot of these little towns have these signs in the outfield, you know, if you hit the sign, even if you're on the visiting team, you got a steak. They'd give you a certificate for a steak or a steak dinner because these weren't Kansas City people, they weren't ranchers. They were car dealers or something like that.

And so, long story short, there was this girl that I met in Montreal the season before. She was white. We had a few days off in Winnipeg and I just wanted to see the Montreal Canadians—they were my favorite hockey team. I'm a big sports guy. And I met this girl—Judy. She was very nice. I asked her how to get to the stadium and we eventually became good friends. Strictly platonic. And this ties into Waterloo and Wisconsin Rapids because she wanted to know where she might run into me again. And I said, "Well, I don't know where I'm going but I'll give you my number. I'll give you our schedule and I'll give you a jingle if I'm ever back in Canada again."

So anyway, the next spring I gave her a call. She was going to be visiting a cousin in Wisconsin Rapids, which was on our schedule. So I said, "I'll leave two tickets. Even though we're visitors. I think I might be able to get tickets for you and your cousin." So I leveraged some tickets for her and her cousin to come to the game. And I doubled and hit a home run off the sign. So I got two kegs of beer. That's the kind of stuff they'd do. You know, two kegs of beer for the team. Take it back to the hotel. Have some drinks, you know.

So I won that and I said, "Hey, why don't you bring your cousin to the hotel and I can introduce you to some of my teammates, coach, managers, stuff like that." And she was thrilled. She was like a little kid. She liked baseball. I said, "Come up if you want, or I'll come down to the lobby and I'll bring some of the fellows." She decided to come up. Just her; her cousin stayed down in the lobby. And she knocked on a door but it wasn't my door. It was the door of a guy on our team from West Virginia. A big guy. About 6 foot 2. His door was not exactly across from mine but kind of staggered a little bit to the right. But she thought it was my door and when he opened it she said, "I'm here to see Johnny. John Thompson, the baseball player." And I'm going to get into it now. He said to her, "You need to stick with your own kind. Why you want to be running around with a Black" and then the "N-word."

And man, I heard that. I heard all of it. She ran down the hall sobbing, just crying. And I said to this guy, "I heard what you told her. She was a friend, just visiting a relative. Why would you say something like that?" "Because she shouldn't be fooling around with" and once again, he said "Black N-words." So I knocked him out. You know, I'm 5 foot 10, 190, and he had four inches on me, but I put him down. I didn't like that. It was disrespectful. I didn't appreciate what he said, so I lost it.

And through all that commotion, Steve Boros runs down the hall, saying, "What happened?" I told Steve what happened. And Steve says, "We're not going to have any racial issues here." He said that he'd played in the Major Leagues and he'd played in the Minor Leagues and that we all come from different states and parts of the country and that guys are just here to play baseball. Their social life, their private life, shouldn't be anybody else's business. He wasn't going to have it on the team. The next thing I knew, that guy was on a bus to the airport. They released him. I don't know why I did it, but I just . . . what he said . . . It really hurt, you know what I mean? I never heard from that girl again.

In 1971 I went to San Jose to play for Buddy Peterson. Buddy Peterson actually said that he did not like Black ballplayers. And why couldn't we find another position, another job, you know what I mean? Another career. He was tough to play for. I'm looking at my numbers there: Eighty-seven plate appearances. Eighty-one at bats. Runs scored: three. Twelve hits. Two doubles. A triple. No home runs. Seven RBIs. I hit .148 that year.

We had seven, maybe eight, African American players at the start but only three by the end of the season. One of them was Al Cowens. He played with the Kansas City Royals and Seattle Mariners. He passed away at fifty, God rest his soul. Great guy. But anyway, Cowens was playing right. When I was playing, I played left. Tommy Combs from Sacramento was our center fielder. He was white. And what Buddy did was . . . Jim Wohlford. I don't know if you've heard that name. Wohlford made the Major Leagues—he was a second baseman. But Buddy started using Jim in my spot in left field. I don't know why. He platooned me and sometimes he wouldn't play me at all. That really bothered me.

Buddy Peterson was one of the reasons I quit baseball. I didn't get released. I quit. After that season, I called John Schuerholz. Schuerholz was the architect behind the Atlanta Braves. Won something like eleven titles in a row. At the time he was with the Kansas City Royals as player-development manager. I called him on the phone and said, "John, I can't play for Buddy anymore." I didn't want to go back to San Jose. I just went back to college and got my degree. I did play ball after that—summer leagues, semipro teams, stuff like that. But I lost my love for baseball. Buddy just took it out of me.

My career average was only .208. I know I could have been better. Remember, I was still hitting right-handed. But I certainly wasn't going to try to tell them I can hit left-handed.

A year or two later, Rosie Gilhausen still didn't know I had left the team. I saw him somewhere, at a game or something, and he says, "John, how's it going? How're you doing?" And I said, "I stopped playing after my third year." I told him how they wouldn't let me switch-hit. And he says, "Wow. Had I had known that, I would've gotten you on a better team or with another organization. Because Lou Dials was extremely high on you."

The African American players on the team, when it came to Buddy Peterson, we didn't really talk about him to each other. We were each saying to ourselves, I wonder what . . . because each manager had to send a report in on each player after every game back then. And I can tell you, we didn't know what he was putting in our reports. "Well, John's got a bad attitude and he thinks he should play, but his performance doesn't indicate that he should play," I don't know. But I do know that he released at least three of the African American players that season. I want to say three, maybe four; we only ended up with three: Al Cowens, myself, and Art Demery.

In my three years I never had any Black coaches. I think that could have helped, in terms of maybe just pulling a Black coach aside and saying, "Hey, can we go to the cage after the game or practice? I want you to see me hit left-handed" or something like that. Maybe I could have said, "Hey, why shouldn't I hit left-handed?" I think it really hurt me. I was told that first year that I had to hit right-handed, and I had to learn to hit all over again. Because hitting lefty, right, it's all totally different.

So anyway, that's, that's the story of my three years in professional baseball.

As I said, I did play for five or six years after that—semipro ball back with my old coach, Robert Pierce, of the Compton Browns. Then I spent thirty-three years working for Fortune 500 companies, Fortune 50 companies, in sales management. I got my degree from UCLA in marketing and advertising. So everything worked out great after baseball. I coached at Compton High School. I've got some kids that are all-state and all-CIF—California Interscholastic Federation—that I worked with. One kid is going to Kentucky now: Andy Rosales, a left-handed pitcher, who holds all the strikeout records at Compton High. He's got ten brothers and sisters. The five sisters all got their degrees but he'll be the first boy in the family to get his college degree. And he wants me to stand with him at Kentucky's Senior Day. He called me last week. Says, "Coach, I can ask one of my brothers or sisters to come, but you're like a father to me," because he never knew his father. I brought him up real slowly and carefully and helped him out. Andy Rosales is a great kid. Remember that name because I think he might get drafted this year.

11

GLENN STERLING

As a kid I dreamed about baseball every day.
About playing in the Major Leagues.
We played baseball twenty-four seven in the backyard.
We'd watch the World Series,
Imitate the players.
I loved baseball up until the time I actually played it.

I didn't play baseball in high school. I played Little League, junior league, senior league, but I had other interests when I got to high school. I worked at a grocery store. After I got out of high school a friend of mine, Larry Huley, came by the grocery store one day and said he was playing baseball over with a guy by the name of Chet Brewer. Chet Brewer played in the Negro leagues.

Chet Brewer was what's called a bird-dog scout for the Pittsburgh Pirates. And one of my best friends had just made it to the Major Leagues—Derrel Thomas. I went to see Derrel play at Dodger Stadium. And I was really excited, and Larry asked me to come out and play with them on Sundays, with Chet Brewer. So I got my schedule switched around so I could play on Sundays. I was totally out of shape, totally behind. I was probably one of the worst players on the field.

But I worked every day to condition myself. This was a time when I wanted to make a change in my life; I was probably about eighteen, nineteen years old. I worked a full-time job, and when I got off I would go work out every night. If nothing else, I would throw a ball up against a handball court and catch it. I started working myself back into shape. Took about a year or two.

Chet Brewer had a lot of Major League baseball players, guys that he had signed, guys that were playing professional baseball, that would come play with him in the wintertime. And I got to play with them. I started learning a lot about the fundamentals of baseball that nobody ever taught me before.

And I happened to hook up with a guy by the name of Lyman Bostock. He had just signed a contract with the Minnesota Twins. Lyman went to Cal State Northridge and he hadn't played his first two years there because he was participating in the Black Power movement out there. And Lyman walked out on the field in tennis shoes and asked the coach could he get a chance to play. And the coach let him on the team and he ended up going to the Major Leagues.

And there was a guy that lived down the street from me who used to be a scout with the Detroit Tigers. A guy by the name of Dan Crowley. Dan had a game at USC that was the first game of the USC season each year, called the Crowley All-Star Game. Dan surprised me one day when he said, "I'm going to let you play in my game." I said, "What game is that?" He said, "Well, I have a game where all the Major League baseball players come and play for me one day against USC. Sparky Anderson will be our manager and I'm going to put you in the game because I think you can play." I played against Rod Dedeaux at Bovard Field at USC. I went 2 for 4 that day. I played with a whole team full of Major League baseball players. There was a famous Black umpire named Emmett Ashford there, who was calling the bases, and he says to me, "Who do you play for, son?" I said, "I'm not signed." He said, "Hitting like that you will be soon."

They gave me a lot of encouragement. They said, "You should go on and really work at this." Rod Dedeaux's son, Justin, referred me to a junior college called Harbor JC. And I went to Harbor JC here in California, and we went to the state playoffs that year. I got to play a lot that year and developed as a player. One day Mike Brito, who was a scout in the Mexican League—he was later the guy in the white Panama hat with the speed gun at Dodgers games—offered me an opportunity to play in a series of games against the Hermosillo baseball club down in Ensenada, Mexico. Hermosillo was a winter league team made up of Major League players. And I had some good games. He got me down to Mexico where I got a chance to go play in the Mexican League. Later Mike would sign Fernando Valenzuela.

I went to spring training with the Sultanes de Monterrey in 1976. They could only carry five Americans on the team, you know. I got right to the beginning of the season, and then they got a guy from the Chicago White Sox organization so they sent my contract to one of their Minor League teams in a town called Cananea in the state of Sonora, and I played there. I played in all kind of different *invierno*—winter leagues—down there. All sorts of leagues full of players who didn't really get a shot to play here in the States. All of the leagues I played in were independent leagues, not affiliated with baseball clubs here in the States. We were paid between $500 per month to $850 per month in Mexican pesos.

There's not a whole lot on me on Baseball Cube or Baseball Reference and all that because they don't really record a lot of statistics that happened down there. I've tried to look through Baseball Cube but my name is not really on the Internet as far as the professional baseball stuff because I wasn't classified in the system. Unless you got a signed contract with a team here in the United States, you weren't put in Baseball Cube or Baseball Reference.

As an African American, you had to be a superstar or you wouldn't last a day in Mexico. You had to be able to play every day and you couldn't make any mistakes. As I said, these teams could only carry five "imports," meaning that if you were from the Dominican Republic or United States or any other country, you were considered an import. So once they had their five, that was it. You really had to compete on a regular basis.

I remember my first week in Liga Norte de Sonora—I'm playing against guys that had played AA, AAA baseball here in the States. A lot of guys got sent down to the Mexican leagues and they could play. We were playing 1–0, 2–1 ball games every night. Very tight games. And you could not make a mistake. You had to be on your game all the time. I remember hitting the ball hard every night and going something like 0 for 20. I was hitting line drives, but these guys knew how to play. And I remember being very worried about getting released because I didn't have any hits. And then I remember driving the ball up the middle and getting a base hit. And then I went 30 for 60 and brought my average back up.

Everybody was fighting to get a chance to come up or come back up. A lot of guys had been up in the States and got released and now they're down there playing. And a lot of guys like myself were trying to come up 'cause we didn't get a contract here. And then you had the Mexican players—they'd been playing since they were twelve years old. They were good. They could play.

You learn how to survive. It's a survival process. It's not a cherry walk, it's not something I would recommend for somebody who wants everything—a bed of roses, you know what I mean? Because the conditions are not that great. We traveled sometimes in school buses. Sometimes we traveled in taxicabs. And we stayed in raggedy hotels. It was quite an experience. You have to pick up the language, pick up the food, pick up what to ask for. You pick up . . . you probably pick up more bad words than good words.

I remember the first day of spring training in Monterrey. Normally you would have a cooler or something in the dugout. They bring a tin can of water, and they put ice cubes in it. You know, everybody gets a cup and then you get some water. As I said, it was an experience. But when you have desire and want to do something, you'll pretty much go through anything to do it.

There are all sorts of things you see in Mexico that you don't see here in the States. In Monterrey, Babo Castillo was one of my roommates. Babo would go on to play with the Los Angeles Dodgers and the Minnesota Twins. His name was Bobby Castillo but people called him Babo. Anyway, the police chief came and took Babo and me out one night. And the thing that was really shocking was that he was the police chief of Monterrey. And he took us to his house—he had a picture of me on his refrigerator—and I looked down at the floor. And the floor was dirt. He had a house built on dirt. I had never seen that before. These people were very poor. But they didn't care. To them they were living like kings.

The people in Mexico were very competitive, but I can't say that they were racist. But it was very emotional. You didn't want to lose; you didn't want to be the home team and lose because you might get run out of town. You could be the goat who made the error, you know. But there were times I'd get a home run and win the game and they'd come down out of the stands and swarm you. One time they carried me around and threw money at me. I made a hundred dollars that day. All because I hit a home run.

I was a first baseman and I used to catch as well. I played down there for two or three years until it got to a point where I didn't really see a future in either getting a chance to go to the Major Leagues or the American Minor Leagues. I thought this was going to get me a shot at baseball in America but what happened was, I think it was the third year I went down there, I was really hitting—about .295 or .300. But then I had a couple of bad games and then I pulled a rib-cage muscle and got a knock on the door one morning and they said, "Here, this is your unconditional release." And that meant that I had find another team to play for if I was going to keep playing. I had to make some decisions as to what I wanted to do with my life moving forward. Was it time to give it up or was it time to keep pursuing the dream? I decided at that time that I was going to try to do something else.

I was twenty-three, twenty-four years old. I went into the ministry, but I also stuck around baseball and saw different things that were going on. I was kind of bitter about a lot of things that went on in baseball so I didn't really have an interest in getting involved in coaching and stuff like that. Instead, I started learning business and eventually I became a player agent.

I invented a board baseball game called Businessman's Baseball. Businessman's Baseball dealt with being the owner of a baseball team and becoming rich. The winner of the game became the richest owner after nine innings. You would pick a team and pay money for the superstar players. It was like a Monopoly baseball game. We got the game copyrighted, fully produced, and took it to market. And then they came

out with those handheld computer games and blew us out of the market. But that was what sparked my interest in being a sports agent.

Lyman Bostock was my best friend and a great influence in my life. When he became a free agent he took me with him to pick his agent up from the airport one night. I'll never forget it. And his agent took me to the winter meetings in Anaheim at the Hilton Hotel. He took me around, introduced me to some people. I got to see firsthand what it's like to be an agent. I sat in on a lot of these negotiations and saw what happened, you know. I got a lot of information. I took it and put it in the baseball game.

I got to meet a lot of people—Ted Turner, Charlie Finley. And, I said, I wouldn't mind doing this someday. So later on, I represented a handful of guys that were Minor League players. I had a couple that were AAA but none got to the big leagues.

There were a lot of things that I knew, that I saw, that I could pass on to them. And there were a lot of business things I could pass on to them too, as far as safe investments, stuff like that. But we never really got to that part because they never got to make the money they could've made.

I always encouraged these guys, and always told them that a lot of times they'd hear stuff from management that's not true. A lot of stuff from management—they'd lie a lot, especially with the players they didn't want. For some reason they'd get vendettas against them or whatever. You know, somebody at one place didn't like you. So his friend is a scout. Let me give you an example.

Let's say a scout with the Red Sox doesn't like you. All right. When he sits down with his friend, another scout, he'd say "Oh, don't sign him. Don't do this. Don't do that. He's got a bad attitude." And then the other scout would look at you in a different light than who you are.

I always tried to teach my players. I'd say, "You have to watch everything that you do because you are under a magnifying glass. If you go to a bar and have one drink and five people see you, you've had five drinks. So you have to be careful with your lifestyle, be careful with what you do and how you do it because it can come back to bite you. There are people that are always watching that don't want to see you make it. When you get down, you can never show anybody that you're down. You have to keep all that to yourself."

Sometimes they don't want you to succeed because they have other players that they want to succeed and you play the same position. The other player may be a bonus baby—the owner paid big money for him to be there and he may not have made that big of an investment in you. So who's going to win out in the end? He's got to make his money back. The bonus baby is going to be his guy. Why? Because it's a business. It's not just a baseball game.

I would tell these guys—these African American ballplayers—"You're really going to have to bite your tongue. You're really going to have to not get emotional. You're really going to have to work on believing in yourself, on keeping your confidence levels together. Because they're going to try to take your confidence. They're going to put you on the bench after you've had good games. They're going to do little subtle things to you to make you not believe that you can play the way you can play."

I had a player named Cardoza Tucker, who played in the New York–Penn League a few years ago. He was on the bus one night. He's African American and very dark-skinned. And the guys on the bus were saying, joking, hollering out loud: "I bet you can't see Cardoza out there." Cardoza gets angry and then the farm director—they had a Black farm director—tells me, "We can't tolerate any violence, so we have to release him." So my question is, did they release the guys who said, "I bet you can't see Cardoza"? No.

So you have those types of situations that go on. You have Black people that they put in to run baseball, like the baseball academy out there in Compton. You've got Black people that they put into scouting and all that. However, they're held real close. You've got to do what they say to do or else you're gone. You've gotta laugh at their jokes.

That's why Black players are not in baseball. The whole system is still run by this old system, a racist system, and it's going to continue on because it continues to get passed down. I can't say Major League Baseball isn't doing anything. They took the All-Star Game out of Atlanta a couple of years back. They are doing things. Black Lives Matter has opened the door for a lot of vital discussion in those areas, but you're going to have to get a lot of Blacks into positions, maybe not on the field, but into the scouting-supervisor positions or director-of-scouting positions where changes can be made. And you have to get qualified people that can make decisions and not be yes-men. Some of the best decisions are made because people disagree. Iron sharpens iron. But when you're told, "You've got to do what I say to do," it doesn't work.

But you also have to look at the colleges, the Division 1 colleges. There are almost no African Americans playing Division 1 baseball. Do you think that's by choice? By African American players? They don't want to play at Stanford? They don't want to play at Florida State or Michigan?

Going forward, I think that the college coaches at the D-1 level are going to have to do a better job of recruiting African American players. Because that's where they get seen, that's the spotlight. They've really got to open the doors at the college level because that's where the training is and nowadays these kids really have to be trained to play. You know, back in my day, you didn't have to be as trained to play as you do now.

I turn on the TV and watch these colleges play. UCLA doesn't have any African Americans on their team. USC has, I think, maybe, one, at best. They need to expand that. They need to give scholarships to these kids. They do that and then you'd have more African Americans in Major League Baseball. They say they can't find African American players who can play at that level. Well look at Lyman Bostock. If Coach Bob Hiegert at Cal State Northridge hadn't allowed him to try out wearing tennis shoes he never would have made it to the Major Leagues and finished second behind Rod Carew for the American League batting title.

Back in the day, you looked at Arizona State—they had Bobby Pate, Kenny Landreaux, Ricky Peters, Hubie Brooks. That's four African Americans right there and they all ended up in the Major Leagues. So that's kind of where the problem is today. There's also the issue of scholarship money. There's not as much of it for baseball as there is for the bigger sports, like football and basketball. But there's a thing called financial aid and a lot of these Black kids will qualify for it because they're coming from low-income backgrounds. So they could get there, you know what I mean? They could get the chance to get there.

There are a lot of African Americans that could play in the big leagues if they could get the right chance. Just the right break. It takes an opportunity. Just one opportunity can make it happen. Like Fernando. He came from Mexico. It was Al Campanis who signed Mike Brito, basically to find him a Hispanic player who could fill the upper decks of Dodger Stadium. And because of that, they did something extraordinary. They found Fernando Valenzuela.

I don't hold any grudges and I'm not saying that I didn't make it because I was discriminated against, because that wasn't the case at all. I wasn't really concerned with who liked me and who didn't. I was going to go out there and do my best anyway. In other words, the racism and all that stuff didn't personally affect me to the point where it affected my ability. But you know it's there and you just gotta go through it. You just deal with it. But I mean, I didn't have to go through the things that maybe Satchel Paige and Cool Papa Bell went through in the South.

As a kid I dreamed about baseball every day. About playing in the Major Leagues. We played baseball twenty-four seven in the backyard. We'd watch the World Series, imitate the players. I loved baseball up until the time I actually played it. But I have a lot of good memories, met a lot of good people. And a lot of the guys that I played baseball with, we're all friends now, good friends. And so we talk about the good old days. I have no regrets. I have no regrets. I got to do something that a lot of people didn't get to do.

12

WIL AARON

> Look in the infield:
> White ballplayer at first
> White ballplayer at shortstop
> White ball player at second
> White ballplayer at third
> And the Blacks
> Are stuck
> In the outfield
> We can't see this?

When I was young I was very close with my cousin Hank. We spoke several times, but then my father migrated from Hayneville, Alabama—Hank was raised in Mobile—to the Los Angeles area and I lost contact with a lot of family. But I did know that Hank was playing baseball, and I had several conversations with him. And I'll share that with you later, as I get into talking about my career and how that went.

But actually, it was my older brother who got me into baseball. He had gotten into it and then I just took it up somewhere around the age of seven. My brother was very athletic and anything that big brother tried, I tried. We roller-skated. We played football. We played basketball. We ran track. We swam. We had skateboards. We did it all.

Eventually I started playing Little League. We played in a legendary Little League in Denker Park. We were outstanding. We beat up teams. We whipped them. And one of the umpires in that league was a tall guy named Ziggy. Ziggy Marcell. He was in the old Jackie Robinson story—the movie that was made in the fifties. He played in the Negro leagues and on the Harlem Globetrotters. And he played basketball with Jackie Robinson.

Later, I played at Manual Arts High School. I was a three-year varsity player. I had outstanding statistics. And I can recall the game that got me drafted. We were playing against LA High School. They had a number of good ballplayers. I remember Victor Harris played for them. He'd go on to play with the Chicago Cubs. I doubled, I dropped a bunt down, I tripled, and I stole a base. And I backhanded a bases-loaded line drive and turned it into a double play. I just had an outstanding game. Everything went right that game.

The league my high school was in had a lot of good players. Danny Ford, who'd play for the California Angels and Baltimore Orioles, played for Fremont. Chester Lemon was there. Derrel Thomas, he was at Dorsey High School. Lyman Bostock. Just a number of outstanding players. Lyman Bostock and I grew up together. We played high school baseball together. He was two years older than me. He always did things right, with the bat. He was an outstanding hitter.

I was drafted by the St. Louis Cardinals out of high school but didn't sign. I went on to LA Valley College, and I played with the Baltimore Orioles' scout team as a junior. One of the things that got me drafted the second time was that I led that team in hitting. And we had a number of top players. Doug DeCinces was on that team. Gary Alexander was our catcher.

Richie Coggins, Rob Andrews. But I was proud to say that I led the team in hitting. And that's one of the things that Ray Poitevint, the Orioles scout who signed me, said was what drove him to draft me. And I was drafted number one in the secondary phase with the Baltimore Orioles in 1971. That's for players that had been drafted before. I was the first pick for the Orioles. I signed for $7,000.

They sent me to Bluefield. Bluefield, West Virginia. In the Appalachian League. Up in the mountains. I enjoyed playing there. But just to fill you in on a few things, I remember there was one guy on the team—a white player. His name was Carl Duncan. I believe he was out of North Carolina, and he was kind of a wild character. He used to pick on me all the time. He was a bully. And, I had a guy that used to always protect me. He was an African American player named Leon Corbin. To this day, I've got a lot of respect for him. He was my protector in rookie ball.

I hit over .300 that season—.315. And I led all third basemen in fielding. One of the things about that league and any league is that if you're playing sixty-two games, which is what we played, you gotta be in shape. And I was not in shape for sixty-two ball games. So I changed a few things after my first year. I used to twist my ankle a lot. I dove back into first base once towards the end of the season and I pulled my thigh muscle. And I remember my manager, Jimmy Schaefer, thought I was shirking my duty because I was sitting out. I was one of the hitting leaders in the league and some felt maybe I was just sitting it out because I had a chance to win the batting title. And I told Jimmy, no, my leg was really, really, sore; it was really bothering me.

But he gave me a little flak about that so I went in. I went in to play and miraculously turned a double play towards the end of the game. I don't know how I did it. And I was in the shower after the game and Jimmy Schaefer looked at my leg and he said, "Jesus Christ, man, why didn't you tell me?" My leg was actually purple and was so swollen I couldn't bend it.

And so that's one of the first inclinations I got about how they viewed African American players. They think they're shirking or they're lazy, or they don't want to play, and they don't understand. But when Jimmy Schaefer saw my leg, he was quite shocked: "Man, why didn't you tell me?" I said, "I tried to tell you."

In 1972, I went to Lodi in the California League. A ball. I tied a California League record that year by getting eleven consecutive hits. Garry Maddox had set the record a year earlier. He ended up marrying the sister of one of my best friends. But anyway, one of the things I learned as I journeyed through baseball was that white players get away with a lot of things that African American players can't get away with. And some things that they did, if an African American player had done it, he would have been out of baseball. For instance, we had a ball game in San Jose, where the Kansas City Royals had a team. They had Al Cowens, George Brett, John Wathan, Frank White. I remember we were rolling into San Jose, and I'm not gonna call out any names but there were some ladies in a car and some of the white guys on our club stood up in the bus, rolled the windows down, and stuck their behinds out of the window. And I was just thinking to myself, like, this is crazy. I mean, how do you get away with stuff like this? I would never dream of doing anything like that, but it was stuff like that that the white players did, and they got away with it. And I never forgot that. I'm a coach right now, and I teach players how to act. You know, what to say, what not to say. Be careful what you say on social media, and how to behave yourself. But I've seen some wild things that I would never dream of doing. But I'll always remember a couple of white players getting up and sticking their behinds out of the bus windows to a couple of girls that were riding right alongside us.

And then I moved on, playing in Asheville, North Carolina. AA baseball. Asheville was an awakening for me because this was the first time I had really seen good pitching. You know, guys were throwing sliders and stuff. And I just wasn't ready. I hit a lot of good balls right at people. And I ended up having, I thought, a bad year. I hit .256.

In '74 I played in the Texas League. It was there I hit .324. I had nine triples. I was within the top five in the league in hitting, and we had a number of top players in that league: Jack Clark, Larry Herndon, Bruce Bochy. It was just flooded with great players. Larry Anderson and Dennis Eckersley were on my team and let me tell you, Dennis Eckersley just had that aura about him. He was good and he knew he was good. I liked him; he played with fire. I played hard all the time but I enjoyed doing my best for Larry and Dennis. They had "Can't Miss" signs on them. I just loved the way they played the game, and how competitive they were.

I had a revelation in my game that year. I roomed with Orlando Gonzalez, who was the top stolen-base leader in the nation, out of the University of Miami. He was Cuban. And he told me one day: "Willie," he said, "if I had your speed, I would, I would lead the league in stolen bases." And I said to myself, Why am I not leading the league in stolen bases? Here's a guy that's telling me I should be.

It was at that moment that I began to be a student of the game. I began to study the game. I studied hitting. I studied fielding. I studied throwing. I studied it all. I watched players, and I learned all that I could learn. I learned how to run the bases coming out of the batter's box. I learned how to round the bases—hit the front part of the bag, turn to the inside. I learned to pay attention to which way the wind was blowing, where were the infielders, where are the outfielders, what inning is it, what's the score, how to take leads—never cross over with your left foot. All of this. I remember doing all these things. And I studied hitting. I studied Carew. I studied the top hitters. I read books on Sadaharu Oh.

I studied all of this. I studied my cousin, Hank Aaron. And I put it all together in 1974. I learned that all of the great hitters keep their hands to the inside part of the ball. All of the great hitters, the ones that drive the ball and hit for extra-base hits, they know how to get the ball slightly up in the air, get the ball over the infielders' heads. So I was faced with, when you keep your hands to the inside, do you do like Matty Alou and swing flat? Or do you chop at the ball? Or do you learn to get slightly up under the ball and go to the inside? The most effective way of hitting is to bring the hands to the inside part of the ball, and you get the ball up in the air. You have to go to the gaps, hit home runs. If you can't do that, you can't play at the higher levels of baseball. The infielders are too good.

So I learned to hit a lot of extra-base hits and go for the gaps, get my legs in shape, and run pole to pole. Ten pole-to-poles before each game. I got my legs in shape to run triples. I wasn't going to go out and run five thirty-yard sprints and call myself ready. When the season was over, I was ready to play again because my legs were in shape. That's when I learned how to play the game. And once I learned that, I was ready.

But there were a lot of politics of what I went through about the position I played. There's a thing called position displacement which takes place in professional baseball and it systematically excludes African Americans from the game. In other words, we're talking about 5, 6, 7 percent of African Americans playing the game on the Major League level, which is what we're seeing today. And most of them are dumped in the outfield. I was 5 feet 8, 5 feet 9, 152 pounds when I broke in, and played at that weight for three years. Eventually I went up to 160 pounds. You don't take guys that are five eight, five nine, 160 pounds and move them to the outfield. Out there, I'm not suited, really. And the first thing they say when they move them out there is because of speed. This is why you have 5 percent, 6 percent, African Americans playing the game: because the doors aren't open for them to play second base, shortstop, pitcher, catcher. You haven't had an African American working catcher since what, the 1990s? Charles Johnson? Early 2000s?

I was a second and third baseman. I was a top fielder in 1971. In 1972 I was moved to the outfield when I went to the California League. Couldn't get back in the infield. I was a shortstop in high school. I was a shortstop in college. I was a shortstop when I was drafted. You don't take guys at five eight, five nine, and 160 pounds, and get mad at them because they can't play center field and hit thirty home runs. You won't last long when you're measured against guys like Barry Bonds. You won't last long when measured against guys that are legitimate home run hitters.

I expressed this to the Orioles: "Give me a chance to play second base," I said. And they traded me over to Cleveland. It was to get a chance to play second base, I was told. But my first day of spring training with the Cleveland Indians, I'm working out at second base, and Bob Quinn, the farm director, calls me in and says, "Wil, I want you to work in the outfield." And I said, "My impression was, I thought it was going to get a chance to play second base. That's why I was traded." "Yeah, you're going to get a chance, but for now, I want you to go to the outfield."

So I was moved to the outfield. Finally, during my 1975 season I got a chance to play a little second base. I played seventy-four games at second and played it well; made four errors. And then they moved me back to the outfield. One day we rode into Amarillo for a doubleheader. And Bob Quinn, the farm director, was in town. There were a lot of scouts that were inquiring about me, and they would ask, "Why isn't Wil playing second base?" And Quinn said, "Oh, Wil can't play second. He can't play second base."

I'm going to share some deep thoughts here, and it hurts me to get into this again because it brings back bad memories. But I went to the outfield before the second game of that doubleheader and went behind the fence and I cried like a baby. I cried like a baby as a result of what was happening to me. I had no control over it. Over anything.

I came back the next year and they sent me to A ball. San Jose. I played there two weeks and hit .381. And they brought me back up to Williamsport. AA ball in the Eastern League. I was starting a little bit, and I was finally playing second base. Then Bob Quinn brought up a kid that I was alternating with in A ball that year—Rico Bellini. He was hitting .233. He stuck that kid in front of me.

And let me back up a little bit. The only reason I got the job playing second base at Williamsport was because I played with a dear friend on that team, his name was Glenn Redmon. He played a little bit with the San Francisco Giants. One day I was taking ground balls. I'm working out at second with Glenn, who was our starting second baseman. Glenn was a little bit older—twenty-eight, and he was white. And Glenn says, "Why aren't you playing second base?" I said, "Glenn, let me tell you what's going on, what I've been going through." Glenn was pissed. And the next day, Glenn quit. He took off, left, and went back to Phoenix, Arizona. He went back to Phoenix so that I could get a chance to play second base. I'll never forget this. He took off and became a schoolteacher. I took over and was playing second base.

And then we rolled into Quebec for a series and that's when Quinn brought up Rico Bellini.

So I was back to playing left field; they moved me from second base back to the outfield. And I was filled with frustration. Like, year after year this is going on, and I'm not getting the chance to play my natural position. I came up to bat, I was leading off against Mike LaCoss, who would go on to pitch with the Giants. Shoot, shoot, shoot, shoot—struck out on four pitches. And I walked back to the bench. The crowd was all "Booo, booo!" I went down to the end of the bench, the far end of the bench. And I said to myself, These people think that I can't play. They think that I can't hit, listen to them. And I said, Okay. I said, Showtime, go with your best.

I walked up to the plate the next time. I said, I'm going right up here, left-field line. Wham! Up the left-field line, base hit. Took off for second. Safe. Next pitch stole third base. Catcher threw the ball into left field, and I scored. I came up the next time. I said, I'm going right between the left fielder and the center fielder. Whack! Right between the left fielder and the center fielder. Double. Came up the next time, I said, Okay, he's going to work me inside because I went twice toward the opposite field on him. Threw me a fastball inside, I whacked it, in the corner for a triple. Next time up, I'm looking for a fastball. I'm gonna square up on him. And here comes a fastball up the middle, and I almost took his head off. I went four for five.

And this is one of the lessons I try to teach kids. Nobody knows what you're going through. All they know is that you walked up there and you looked bad, and you struck out on four pitches. So I always tell kids, "When you get your chance, do it! Stay ready. Nobody knows what you're going through." So I kind of learned that that day. I learned how to continue to fight, continue to put on a display, continue to perform, in spite of the negative things I was going through.

I finished within the top five that year in hitting. I was second in the league in stolen bases with thirty-four. There were only four .300 hitters in the league besides me: Andre Dawson, Larry Murray—Eddie's brother, Pedro Guerrero, and Steve Henderson. They all went to the big leagues, except for me.

I got so frustrated I drove down to Memorial Stadium in Baltimore one day. I spoke with Frank Robinson, who was managing the Major League Cleveland Indians club at the time. They were in town so I drove to the stadium and went into the clubhouse there and spoke with him. He was amazed that they didn't even send him my stats. He said, "You hit

.300 and they didn't call you up? And they never even sent me your stats?" He had a few newsmen, writers, around him. And I was kind of scared to say what I really wanted to say to him. And he said, "You ask Quinn why he's not giving you an opportunity." And then he took me aside and said, "You get the hell out of this organization because it's racist." When Frank Robinson told me that I knew I wasn't going to sign my contract and come back with them the next year. I refused to sign my contract and I was blackballed out of baseball.

I never got a chance to play baseball again. I contacted Rosie Gilhousen, who was a big scout with the Kansas City Royals. He had seen me play in the LA area. I contacted Rosie and he said, "Send me your material." He was going to get me with Kansas City. I was gonna go with the Royals. Then Rosie gets back to me and he says, "Jesus Christ, Wil, what did you do over there—beat somebody up?" He said, "They got the word out on you." He was the first one to tell me that I was blackballed.

So, I understand situations. I understand. I'm much older now. I understand Kaepernick. When you stick your neck out, when you do that and you talk about the racial issues, they'll want you out. I understand this fully.

I called Ray Poitevint right after my season was over, in which I hit .308. I said, "Ray, you got to help get me out of this situation." I told him about not getting a chance to play second base and how they dumped me in the outfield and played games with me. He said, "Wil, I think you're blowing this infield thing all out of proportion." I said, "Ray, I'm not seventeen years old anymore. I understand what's going on. I've been in spring training every year. I see the number of African Americans in the game. I see where they're playing." Ray tells me, Okay, he's going to make plans to get me. Then he calls me back, and you know what he says? He couldn't get me. He was the farm director for the Milwaukee Brewers, the scout who signed me, and he wouldn't touch me.

So what I'm trying to tell you is that it's a pattern. It's a pattern that has been going on. It is not a pattern that has just started. There's a few that slipped in. I had a talk with Garry Templeton when he was playing in the Minors. I said, "Garry, let me tell you." I said, "If you stay at shortstop you can be on the All-Star team. You can probably go to the Hall of Fame. But if they move you to the outfield, things can change."

I had a talk with Ron Washington. Ron Washington was a second baseman in the Dodgers organization who was playing in Waterbury. They were moving Ron Washington from second to third, and they would tell him he couldn't play second. I said, "Ron, you can play second. You have a pro flip. They just don't want you to play second. You got to understand what's going on." And he kind of looked at me, bamboozled, like, really? I had to emphasize to him that he could play second because he had lost confidence. He got traded to Minnesota and went on to play second base and played a number of years in the big leagues at second base. But the Dodgers were telling him he couldn't play second.

There are numerous stories I have of where this has happened, to a number of players. And I think why my story is so legit is because when they gave me an opportunity to play, I performed. You can't say you released me because I couldn't hit. You can't say you released me because I couldn't run or anything. I hit over .300 three years out of my six professional seasons, and twice in AA. Bob Quinn made a promise in 1976 during spring training. He said, "Any person who hits .300 in the Eastern League will be in the big leagues. I guarantee you." I said, Okay. I hit .300, was never called up. Was never called up.

I called my cousin, Hank Aaron, right after the '76 season. Called him from Williamsport and explained to him, "Hey, I just hit .300 in the Eastern League. Can you help me get out of this organization?" He said, "You hit .300 in the Eastern League?" He said, "It feels like they would have called you up just for hitting .300." I said, "They didn't call me up. So, I mean, are you denying I hit the .300? I hit the .300, but I'm telling you, Hammer, they didn't call. I'm telling you." He asked me to call him back in five minutes. I called him back. They said he was in a meeting. I called him back several other times. They said he was still in the meeting. And you know what, he never returned my call. He never returned my call. I just thought, Well maybe you can make a phone call over to somewhere and see if you could maybe get me a tryout to go somewhere else. I guess it was just too much pressure on him to attempt to do anything. But not to return the phone call?

Do you realize that I still have nightmares? I still have dreams of running to catch the train with the baseball team, and I missed the train. I'm playing in the outfield. I'm playing, and I'm running through quicksand. And I don't have my uniform. It's in the cleaners. The cleaners is closed. I still have nightmares, and I'm trying to get over this now. It would be easy for me to say I wasn't good enough. Hey, you didn't hit good enough. You weren't good enough. Hey, come on. I was good enough. But I was denied an opportunity to strut my stuff.

I went to Venezuela after the '76 season. I played summer ball there. I hit .339. I was, I think, third in the league in hitting. I led in five offensive categories, set a record—most stolen bases in a game with five. I was the Most Valuable Player. I got a chance to play winter ball and played one game with Dave Concepcion. He was at second base, I think, for Aragua. I swiped three out of four stolen bases. And I remember when

I stole one, Concepcion said, "Jesus Christ, what team do you play for?" I said, "Yeah, I was with Cleveland." And I began to explain to him briefly what had taken place. He said, "Oh yeah, they do that. I understand what you're saying. I know where you're coming from. They do that." That's what he told me.

I was always taught by my mother and father, you work hard, you be the best, you get the job, you get rewarded. But it doesn't work like that. We gotta quit telling our kids that. It doesn't work like that. It doesn't.

Lyman Bostock, we grew up together, a few blocks away. We played high school ball together. We played junior league baseball together. He called me in Venezuela. He said, "The California Angels, they're looking for a second baseman because Bobby Grich hurt his back." He got the okay, supposedly from Buzzie Bavasi, to call me. So I flew in, Lyman picked me up, we worked out. Worked out and played in some games and stuff before spring training. I helped Lyman move into his house, in Los Angeles. And, when I was there he got a phone call from Buzzie Bavasi. And, Buzzie Bavasi asked Lyman, was it all right if I come to Minor League spring training camp because he had a few guys he wanted to look at, Dickie Thon and Floyd Rayford. And Lyman agreed. And we argued for days. I said, "Lyman." I said, "if you don't stick to this, man, and make sure that I'm in camp," I said, "it's going to be over." He said, "No, no, no. You'll go down to AAA." He said, "You'll go to AAA, you'll go to Salt Lake City, and you'll win the batting title." I said, "Okay."

I went 10 for 21, went down there, with two home runs, one grand slam, 8 out of 8 stolen bases, 11 RBIs. Mike Port calls me off of the field into the clubhouse one day. We're getting ready to play the AAA San Diego Padres. And he said, "Wil, I just wouldn't be telling the truth if I didn't say that you came here and knocked the cover off the ball. But we're going to go with the younger ballplayers." He told me that, after I had been going through this, year after year after year, in the California League and the Texas League, the Eastern League, and Venezuela, trying to prove myself. But it doesn't matter what you do, or how good you perform. It has nothing to do with whether you're good enough. "We were hoping for you to have a bad spring training so we could release you," he told me. "But we're gonna release you anyhow." I was twenty-five. I was twenty-five years old, and I was polished. I was polished. I knew what I was doing. I knew how to hit. I knew what I was doing. He said, "Well, the Oakland A's are interested in you. And they'd like to you to . . ." Hey look man, you don't tell somebody that's hit .300 in the Eastern League, .300 in the Texas League, Most Valuable Player in summer ball, and then winter ball to go try out. I know what's going on.

This is what happened. This is a true story. I haven't been drinking. I'm not on drugs. This is true. This is what happens. This is how they do it. If you don't understand what's going on, you can start drinking. You can start doing drugs because you think you're inferior, you're not good enough.

So, you know what I began to do? I began teaching. I began training kids. I coached the Dodgers' scout team. We whipped up on teams. I coached the Detroit Tigers' scout team. Then, I went into high school coaching. That's all I do now, is coach. I vent myself now by teaching and training. Training kids, teaching them to be better. If I didn't get a chance, somebody else is gonna get a chance.

Ask yourself, Why aren't there more Black second basemen or shortstops? We had a lot coming up through the Negro leagues. There was a whole lot of them. Why is it that we can't play the quarterback position and shortstop? Those are the thinking positions. They denied African Americans for years an opportunity to play quarterback. Now those doors are open. But baseball . . . baseball has yet to change.

The first thing they say, when they're dumped in outfield, is that it's because of their speed. Well, I don't buy it. It's called stacking. Stack them all in the outfield, and don't give them a chance to play infield. And then you want to know why the numbers are low. It's still done today. They took Mookie Betts, who came up as an infielder and they moved him to the outfield. He was a second baseman. And he's in the outfield, right field, doing a good job. But how many guys can make that jump and hit twenty-five or thirty homeruns at 5 feet 9, 175 pounds?

What would Ozzie Smith have looked like as a center fielder? What would Ron Washington look like playing left field? What would Garry Templeton have looked like? Maybe they'd do an average job, but they wouldn't be the star players that they were.

When I talk to the kids, the first thing I tell them is you have to be trained. If you want to learn to play shortstop, you want to learn to play second base, you gotta know what you're doing. You gotta know how to do the flips. You got to know how to do the pivots. You gotta know how to come around the bend. You gotta know how to field slow rollers. You gotta be smart. You gotta know the rules. Ball's popped up to the infield, second base calls it, the first baseman calls, pitcher calls, whose ball is it? It's the second baseman's ball because he's in charge. He has the right of way. Okay. Then after that, you gotta know the politics. That you don't have any control over it.

I told MLB when they asked, "Look, we need more Black ownership in baseball. We need more Black general managers. We need more Black scouts with the power to sign. We need more Black college coaches that'll give kids a chance to play.

Because if the doors are closed you don't get in. If the doors are closed, it's simple. No matter how good you are, you don't get in." As Tony Gwynn said, "You can't do anything if you're not given an opportunity." There needs to be more inclusion. And right now, there's no inclusion. Now, we can try to pretend. We can try to pretend like, Oh, you just weren't good enough. Or, We just can't find any Black shortstops. We've got Tim Anderson, but he's the only guy. Really? Come on.

I listen to Black parents talking about their kids who are in school. I hear them saying, "My kid, he's not getting a chance to play shortstop." Duh! I went through this in the seventies. It's still going on. And, "They put him in the outfield. They say, 'Oh, because of his speed; he runs fast.' He's a shortstop. He's never even played outfield." And then you look in the infield: white ballplayer at first, white ballplayer at shortstop, white ballplayer at second, white ballplayer at third, and the Blacks are stuck in the outfield. We can't see this?

You walk into spring training, two or three Blacks in the organization. And let me say this: I did a frequency distribution when I played. A frequency distribution of where each and every Black played in AAA, of where each and every Black played in the Major Leagues. You can see the pattern. Rochester: zero Black third basemen, zero Black shortstops, zero Black second basemen. The Major League club, zero, zero, zero. Go to each organization, do a frequency distribution, and you'll get your answer. Look in the college ranks. Listen to the Major League draft: such and such African American kid, shortstop out of Texas. Oh yeah, they're going to move him to the outfield. Oh yeah, yeah, he's going to be a good outfielder. Really? Really? Never give him a chance to even play.

And we want to know why it's 7 percent African American, and of the 7 percent, they're all stacked in the outfield. And we want to know why the numbers aren't increasing.

13

CHUCK STONE

> It looked
> Like half the town
> Came in
> To watch me get a haircut.

I was originally drafted by the Orioles. I was what you would refer to as a "draft-and-follow" player. I was going to a school called East Los Angeles College when they drafted me. And because they didn't give me any money to sign I went on to Cal State Northridge where we won the national championship. I was the MVP of the 1970 Division II College World Series.

A draft-and-follow player is when a club gets the rights to you and then they kind of follow you along. And they had until, I believe, sometime in August when they had to sign you. If they didn't your name went back in the draft for the next season. I didn't sign with the Orioles. I got right up to that date and then went up to Cal State Northridge and played there. At the end of that season I signed with Detroit. I knew nothing about the Tigers. In LA I grew up a big Dodger fan.

Baseball was always in me; I'm born with it, I guess. I've got pictures of me in diapers holding up a baseball bat bigger than me. My family were musicians and as a kid I used to play the drums because of my parents but I'd hear kids outside playing baseball and I didn't want to come in and practice any longer. I told my mother, I said, Mom, I don't wanna play the drums anymore. I want to go outside and play baseball. We played every day after school in the street until it got dark.

I joined the Cub Scouts only because I found out the Cub Scouts had a baseball team. Baseball was very big when I was a kid. So much so that a number of guys that I grew up with were drafted in baseball coming out of high school. And that became a goal of mine as well—to get into the baseball draft and become a professional. Derrel Thomas was a neighbor, and he became the first-round draft pick of the Astros.

I grew up in what was called the Crenshaw District. It was a very racially integrated neighborhood. We had Japanese, Blacks, Caucasians, a few Hispanics. And my high school was integrated as well. I was president of my class for three years there. And so, I didn't have a real strong racial-bias type of situation growing up. I just liked baseball players.

I used to like Orlando Cepeda and Don Drysdale, Maury Wills. Jimmy Lefebvre had a real impact on me; he played with the Dodgers and he was Rookie of the Year in '65. He was a switch-hitter. But Pete Rose was my idol. Another switch-hitter. I patterned my play after Pete Rose. I wanted to be able to play like him and have people call me Charlie Hustle. That was my goal.

Anyway, there were these two Orioles scouts: Al Kubski and Ray Poitevint, and I was on their scout team. Enos Cabell was on that team along with some other guys who eventually went into pro baseball. A number of them played at Cal State Northridge. I think five of the guys that I played with on that scout-league team got a pro contract.

If you watched the movie, *Million Dollar Arm*, that was Ray

Poitevint. He was the scout involved in that—the game show where they looked for a pitching prospect in India. I played for his scout team.

We would play other scout teams. These were teams full of college-eligible guys who were playing on these scout teams. We'd travel down to San Diego, to Arizona. It was all kids who were also being scouted by one team or another. You didn't get paid for this. It's still done today. You have guys you're interested in signing so you take a look at them. They're predominantly in California. Basically we played on Sundays, some Saturdays.

And then, as I said, I signed as a free agent with Detroit. I decided to drop out of school; left in my senior year. 'Cause like I said, there were kids from my neighborhood or that I played with that were starting to sign. And I started to feel like I was going to be left behind.

A scout by the name of Jack Deutsch called me up one day and asked if I could come up and play with his team on Saturday in a doubleheader. And he says, "Are you sure you can make it to the game?" I said, "Yes, Mr. Deutsch, I'll be there." And he said, "Good, because I want to sign you after the game so be sure to be there." And after the ball game, he took me to his house and I signed with him. I got very little money for signing, I'll say that much. Nothing to write home about. I was just chomping at the bit for the opportunity.

When I got to Lakeland, Florida, where they assigned me, I couldn't believe it was A ball. I said, "Are you kidding me?" It felt like the big leagues to me. We played in all the spring-training parks where the Major League teams played. The hotels were first-class.

It wasn't the pit that people make it out to be. For a guy who wanted to play baseball, I was in hog heaven. I enjoyed it a great deal. My manager in Lakeland was a fellow by the name of Stubby Overmire. He was a little guy like I was, and he liked me quite a bit. He gave me an opportunity because he put me in the lineup as lead-off guy practically every day. I believe I played in 130-something ball games and the schedule was 142. Even when I had a bad day, I'd come back and my name was back in the lineup.

But Florida was a bit of a culture shock because I wasn't accustomed to the Southern drawl, that sort of thing. I couldn't understand people at first—the drawl of the dialect is a lot different than what I was used to out on the West Coast. But I became a bit of a fan favorite because of the way I played—lots of hustle and a lot of fire. And I think that helped me to get accepted by those people who probably wouldn't have accepted me, maybe, because of my race.

But I got along with everybody and never had any problems even though there were certain elements of that society in the South that you had to deal with. But for me it was really no big deal. I'm a people person. I try to see the good in everybody.

You know, pretty much everyplace that I played, other than in high school, I was always the first Black player to play there. Myself and John Young—he was my best friend. We grew up together. We played in high school together. He was drafted by Detroit. He later founded baseball's RBI [Reviving Baseball in Inner Cities] program—he was the first Black player to play at Chapman College. I was the first Black player to play for Cal State Northridge. So I was used to it and really didn't feel any real pressure. I just ignored a lot of it and kept my head down and kept going, treating everyone with respect.

I would have a lot of telephone conversations with Jack Deutsch during that season in Lakeland and he kind of got me through it. He was telling me what they expected. He'd say, "You play hard. You're Chuck Stone and if you play like you're Chuck Stone, that'll be good enough for everybody."

I was the only Black player on the team. There were Hispanic players who were Puerto Rican; two of them were my roommates. They didn't speak much English so I had to learn to speak Spanish. That's how I became bilingual. And now my wife doesn't speak English so I speak Spanish fluently.

I thought that year was good because I got to play a lot. I grew up mentally, baseball-wise, a great deal. I was disappointed that my average wasn't higher than it was, though. I hit into a lot of hard outs; those were big parks and guys were running down balls pretty good. So it made it a little difficult to have a good average, yet still I was pleased that my on-base percentage was extremely high. I scored a lot of runs.

But it was a pitcher's league. It was High-A, the Florida State League, and I faced a lot of tough pitching. But I was able to survive the entire season and it was a lot of fun for me because I just loved playing baseball. We turned two triple plays that year—I played second base. I think we led the league in triple plays!

When the season ended, they didn't really sit down with you and review your season with you. No, back in those days they didn't really do that. For the most part you would just hope you got a new contract in the mail and maybe even a little bit of a raise in pay. Even though things were tough for me that year I did get a new contract in the mail. I got moved up to the Midwest League, in Clinton, Iowa. And it was hard enough to try to get a little bit of a raise. But I did and then I played that season for a fellow by the name of Jim Leyland, who went on to have a lot of success in the big leagues. I was his lead-off guy as well.

Clinton, to me, was the same as Lakeland. I didn't have many racial problems, but I wasn't a guy who'd go out there intermingling with everybody. So maybe that didn't hurt. And I had experienced that area before. After my freshman year in college, I played in a summer collegiate league called the Basin League, where I played in Rapid City, South Dakota. I was one of maybe ten Black people in that town, maybe in the state.

And I remember that at one point that summer my hair got really long. Usually I'm close-cropped so I said I gotta get a haircut. And I walked past this barbershop about ten times before I had enough nerve to walk in there to ask the barber, who was white, to give me a haircut. Finally I did and he says, "I'm not too sure if my blades are sharp enough, but come on, sit down, I'll cut your hair for you." And I'm in the barber's chair and—it was so funny—it looked like half the town came in to watch me get a haircut.

Another time I got invited to the Kiwanis Club to be a speaker at their lunch. They asked what it was like growing up in Los Angeles during the time of the Watts riots, back in '65. They wanted to know what it was like being Black in Los Angeles with the riots going on. I told them, to be totally honest, it was scary. You had to stay inside because there was a curfew in effect. And my parents were pretty strict about me being a decent guy, that sort of thing, so I didn't go out and loot, none of that stuff. I just wasn't raised that way. Also, my grandmother worked for the LAPD. She was working records and identification, and I didn't want to get in trouble because I would hurt my grandmother.

As far as baseball's concerned, wherever I went—Rapid City, wherever—I was known as a holler guy. They call them holler guys—always chattering, that kind of stuff. Also, I used to like to whistle a lot. Whenever I walked around the town or had to go someplace, in Rapid City or wherever, I'd have kids following me around the town saying, "Hey, are you the Whistler?" And I say, "Yeah, I'm the Whistler." "Can you whistle for us?" That's how I got the nickname, the Whistler—from the kids. And I'd chatter: "Hey, batter batter . . . strike 'em

out!" And then I'd whistle. And so the little kids would hear that, and then all of a sudden when I'd whistle, they'd whistle back. So the announcer would say, "Now batting for the Rapid City Chiefs, number six, the Whistler, Chuck Stone." And everybody starts whistling. I was pretty well accepted in that town, especially after I got the nickname.

After that season I got released from the organization. I was told they had to make room for a guy named Tom Veryzer, who was their number-one draft pick. So that's kind of the way it goes. I was a little bit in shock, but I didn't have high numbers—the batting numbers—I guess that they were looking to have. So that was that. But some years later they offered me a job as Minor League manager in rookie ball.

And I actually signed a contract with them. But I never got to manage. I was technically the first Black manager in the Tiger organization, and I was supposed to go to rookie ball in Florida. But during that year I got divorced from my first wife. And I would've had to be in Florida for a long time. And she wouldn't allow my kids, who were ten and eleven at the time, to come visit me there. They really wanted to come but she refused to let them go. So I had to tell Detroit that I wasn't going to take the job because I didn't want to miss my kids over the full summer. So I had to walk away from that. I didn't want to hurt them. I said, I'll find another baseball job somewhere down the line, but I really want to be with my two children.

I let some years go by because I wanted to make sure I had the visitation, that kind of stuff. I ended up working in insurance. I mentioned John Young, my best friend growing up—I was friends with him since we were both fourteen years of age. One night we were talking and he said, "You know, we used to play in all these parks in LA when we were growing up. There were all kinds of community leagues and stuff." He says, "I pass these same parks today, Chuck, and they're all empty. Nobody's playing baseball. I wanna do something about that." This was in the 1980s. "I want to revive baseball," he said to me. Then it just hit him: "We'll revive baseball in the inner cities," and that became the RBI program that baseball runs today.

It wasn't easy. In LA we'd primarily go to inner-city parks, announce that the RBI was coming there and conducting tryouts for teams. All we had were caps and T-shirts. And a certain amount of kids would show up. Parents would show up and we'd ask the parents to get involved, be coaches of the team, you know, dads who had some level of baseball acumen. And it just kind of grew from there.

Along with the baseball there were programs where they would have kids tutored to try to get their grade point averages high enough to where they would qualify for scholarships. A lot of scholarships were given out to some of these kids. And then John gravitated to where RBI had girls' softball and that just blew up for RBI. Because a lot of girls had nowhere to play. John was pushing these girls to do better because that would get them the recognition from the college coaches and give them scholarship opportunities also.

John would go out soliciting big league players to help him out with the funding. The first guy that really came through for him was Kevin Brown. He donated a million dollars to John for the RBI program. That got him off the ground. And then Major League Baseball caught wind of it, and went Hey, this could be a big deal for baseball. And they donated a lot of money to the RBI program.

Around this time, '87 or '88, a friend of mine, Dennis Lieberthal—his son Mike played in the big leagues—recommended me to be a scout for the Tigers. Dennis was a scout with Detroit and after I'd stopped playing in '72 I'd refer guys to him. I referred a number of guys to him that he signed and eventually he helped me to get a scouting job with the Tigers. But then I started thinking to myself: Why don't I give being an agent a try?

I thought I could be a good one because I know what baseball players are up against and what they need to do. I used to tell my players, "Look, you got any problems with your manager or other players or confrontation with the front office . . . you don't go complaining to them. You let me stand in between the two of you and I'll take care of the problem."

I wanted to become a player's agent. You know, you gotta make money to survive, but I was just trying to influence and get my players to the big leagues. I was able to acquire a number of good players. One of them was a kid named Covelli Crisp. I was his agent when he signed, initially. He became Coco Crisp and played in the Major Leagues. When he was playing rookie ball in Johnson City the kids there thought it was interesting to call him Coco Crisp, you know, after the cereal.

I did that until I got a job with the Houston Astros in 2006. At that point I had to stop doing the agent thing because I'm now working for management. I got the Houston job because a good friend of mine, Enos Cabell, was working for them. And they got into a little bit of a problem racially during the 2005 World Series. They were playing the Chicago White Sox and the NAACP was boycotting them outside of the stadium because they were the first World Series team in decades to not have a single Black player. And so the owner got kind of offended by that and he said I have to do something about that because I'm not a racist. His name was Drayton McLane and I liked him a lot.

So Enos Cabell said to him, I know a guy who could help us solve that problem. This guy's name is Chuck Stone. He lives in LA. He could go into the Black community. He can also go into the Hispanic community because he's bilingual. So they asked me to come to the winter meetings that were in Anaheim that year.

So I went to the Anaheim Hilton. They interviewed me, told me what the situation was. They said they would like for me to find minority players in the inner city. I told them it'd be no problem. I'd love to do it. So they hired me and that was my objective, but I was going to look at everybody.

I ran the Astros' scout team from 2006 to 2009. In three years of playing in the scout league against the other scout teams, we lost two games. We beat everybody up pretty bad. And my scouting director, he came out to California to watch us play.

And he hears all this cheering and all these guys—my Astros—running the bases all the time. So he came down to the field where we were. He said, "Chuck, what the hell is going on here?" I said, "We just keep running these guys off the field." And he sees us scoring runs. And I said, "Well, I'm going to keep this job or I'm going to lose it. We've got some n——s on this team. We've got some Mexicans and we got some hard-ass white boys and we come every day to kick your blankety-blank." And he says to me, "Well damn Chuck, why isn't every club that way." So we hit it off real good after that. 'Cause he saw that I wasn't just . . . because I was hired to find blacks and minorities. And I thought I found some pretty good ones, but the whole deal was, we didn't want to look like we were prejudiced in one way. At least that's the way I saw things. So that's what we did.

But my supervisor was very racial. I don't care to mention his name, but he told me to my face one time that he would never sign a Black ballplayer. And then I saw what the problem was for the Astros. They had a lot of kids who could've signed with the Houston Astros during that time, but they weren't being scouted correctly. When I was growing up, heck, the Astros were loaded with Black players, and they'd beat the hell out of you. When I was playing in the Florida State League, they had a team in Cocoa Beach and, man, the Astros had some studs, they could do a number on you. So I was surprised when I found out that they didn't usually sign Black players anymore because of this area supervisor.

For me it was an eye-opener because I always said, Woah, the Astros, they're loaded. They always had a lot of Latin players in their rotation, mixed in with a lot of white players who were good prospects. But this supervisor . . . it's just unfortunate that he didn't pull the trigger on those prospects because we had some guys on our scout team that he just refused to come out and scout and co-sign the deal. Because you know, when you turn a guy's name in as an area scout, the supervisor has to cross-check it. He has to agree with it. I had a lot of trouble with him in that regard.

And then they fired me. I was told I'd have a job for life. That's what I was told when they hired me. But they let me go. Eventually the supervisor got fired too.

When I look back on my days in the Minor Leagues, it's the friendships I remember most. For the most part, I look at it as more of a positive than a negative. I take a little pride in it all. I wear my Detroit stuff whenever I can. People, they might think I'm a little weird out here in California: "What's that D stand for? Dodgers?" I say, "No sir, it stands for Detroit."

I sometimes dream in baseball but those dreams are kind of unfulfilled. And so I try to inspire the youngsters I work with now. I'm too old to play, but I try to inspire them, tell them what it's like in the Minor Leagues, what you need to do to get there, and what scouts are looking for. It gets them to play a little bit harder to try to reach their goal. The goal I was never able to reach.

AFTERWORD

A Note on Method

In his 1966 preface to *The Glory of Their Times*, Lawrence Ritter allows his readers a peek behind the curtain, describing for them just how he managed to corral and set forth the oral histories that followed.[1] Once the grueling hard work was accomplished and he was able to first find and then convince the ballplayers he interviewed to indeed speak to him about their baseball lives, he proclaimed, the rest was easy. So easy, in fact, that Ritter admitted to being a bit sheepish at being labeled the author of the book. "Of course, this book was really not 'written' at all," he alleged. "It was spoken. . . . My role was strictly that of catalyst, audience, and chronicler. I asked and listened, and the tape recorder did the rest."[2]

Needless to say, Ritter spent hours with his subjects, his tape recorder whirring the entire time. (By his own estimate he recorded over a hundred hours of interviews.)[3] What about that? Other than eliminating his questions, rearranging and condensing the material a bit, "I have done very little editing of the tapes," he contended.[4] If so, then what emerged on the pages within the book was indeed a miracle—compelling narratives and heartfelt reminiscences, with almost perfect factual recall of events that had sometimes taken place more than a half century earlier.

The passage of time, however, aided by Ritter himself, has rendered the seemingly miraculous a bit more mundane, at least at first glance. Ritter was hardly protective of the raw material that comprised his masterwork and portions of the audiotapes wound up in the collections of both the Hesburgh Library at the University of Notre Dame and the Giamatti Research Center at the National Baseball Hall of Fame. Curious researchers have dipped into them from time to time to see just how much of those hundred-plus hours of audiotape wound up in the pages of *The Glory of Their Times* and how neatly the raw audio and the written word lined up. As it turned out, Ritter was working a lot harder than he admitted, transforming the choppy, sometimes meandering narratives into a magnum opus of baseball art on the page.

As Rob Neyer, one of those curious researchers, wrote in his *Big Book of Baseball Legends*, Ritter often added details to the stories he was told, rendering them more colorful, more vibrant, more alive.[5] He'd add words that were never uttered by this old-timer or that one but which Neyer posits that Ritter presumed he might use.[6] In the end, at least insofar as Ritter's insistence that he was little more than mere scribe and nominal editor of *The Glory of Their Times*, methinks it a case of the author of perhaps the greatest baseball book ever written—and in the end, there's little debate that it was written and not merely spoken—doth protesting too much.

Neyer reached the same conclusion. "Ritter's done a masterful job of editing this story," he wrote after comparing a selection of the audio and written narrative of Hall of Famer Sam Crawford, "but one can hardly say that he has done 'very little editing,' or that he has 'merely selected and rearranged the material' here."[7] As for why Ritter massaged things the way he did we can only speculate. Neyer posited that it was perhaps Ritter's affection for and admiration of the players he met in his seventy-five-thousand-mile journey across America to find and speak with them and he simply wanted them to "come across well" on the page.[8] Perhaps. But maybe there was more to it than simply that.

Ritter, himself, came clean shortly before his death in 2004 when he admitted in a SABR *Baseball Research Journal* article that his earlier assertion that it was his tape recorder that deserved the bulk of the credit for the glory on the page that became *The Glory of Their Times* was "a misstatement."[9] "Of course there was a lot of work that went into arranging the various elements," he added. After poring over the transcription of the raw audio, "I would begin to hear the voice, its cadence, its peculiarities, so that I could recall its sound and character just by reading the transcript."[10]

Well enough for Larry Ritter, who actually sat down with his subjects and could make the connection between the ear and the page, but this would never do for his readers, who had to rely on the written word, alone, to *hear* the stories rather than just read the words. Ritter, whose day job was as a professor of economics and finance at NYU, was astute enough to realize that for his readers to experience on the page what he had in person, there was a lot of work to do on his part. Perhaps he did in fact want his subjects, many of whom he'd come to befriend, to "come across well," but more fundamentally as a chronicler of a long-bygone era, he understood that it was his duty to honestly and accurately convey his field experience in print if he was to have any hope of succeeding in his endeavor. And it was his job—not his tape recorder's—to figure out how to do this. Obviously, simply printing the transcriptions wouldn't do; anyone who has suffered through hundreds of pages of deposition transcripts could testify to the less-than-optimal reading experience such an ordeal can be. And merely doing what Ritter claimed to do in his original preface—eliminating his questions, condensing and rearranging a bit here and there—would be unsatisfactory as well. The result would be a hodgepodge of stories started and wandering off into the abyss, half-sentences and quarter-formed thoughts. No, what his project required—and what Ritter understood even if he was loath to admit as much—was not so much an editor but a *writer*.

And so he wrote, transforming the raw material contained within the audiotapes into flesh and blood on the page. And the result was, to borrow a word, glorious. In the end, the stories contained within *The Glory of Their Times* are indeed miracles unto themselves, albeit not precisely in the way Ritter's original preface would have had his readers believe.

Which brings me to my soliloquy on the method I employed in putting together the thirteen oral histories contained within this book. How to thoughtfully, honestly, and accurately convey on the page what I heard with my ears during the many hours of interviews with my subjects? What is ethical and what is not? What is fair and what is cheating? There aren't any easy answers here. What initially seemed to me to be a book project that would find me pleasantly on the sidelines as the players themselves took center stage and dictated the narrative very quickly transformed into an ethical morass, one in which I couldn't help but locate myself at the center. From the beginning my intent has always been to do justice to my subjects' stories and present them as I heard them, but as Ritter found over a half century earlier, merely eliminating my questions, condensing and rearranging here and there wasn't going to do the trick. Not by a long shot.

I learned this quite painfully in the afterglow of my first interview. I was on a high after speaking with Mickey Bowers, who was incredibly candid, insightful, and honest about all that he endured as a Minor Leaguer in the Phillies' system in the late 1960s. What I heard was eloquent and moving and I was confident that readers would experience everything I just had with very little additional effort on my part.

Then I read the transcript.

Like Ritter, I could at times *hear* Bowers speak in certain passages of the transcription I was studying, but only sometimes and even then I realized that I could only hear him because I had in fact literally heard him. Readers without a similar leg-up would most likely never hear Bowers at all if I did little more than lightly edit and condense the transcript. The Mickey Bowers that I heard during our talk was living inside the transcript in front of me but he was hiding. And he would remain hidden unless I did some serious work to bring him to the surface.

This, I realized, was to be my job—springing to freedom the voices held captive by the cacophony of words in the transcripts. To someone who has only read oral histories and not written them it might seem counterintuitive to consider the words, themselves, the obstacle to be overcome, but because we speak differently than we write and because we listen differently than we read, this is in fact the case. Or at least this was my experience.

So now I understood what was required of me here. Next came the question of how to do this. And what the guardrails were. Because I had just spoken to Bowers I still had his voice in my head and I realized that this was a key—I had to keep that voice in my head for reference so that I could mold the narrative to the point that I was able to present a suitable facsimile of it on the page. Once I lost the voice I'd lose everything. Yes, I had the recording of our talk but I also had the emotional response his stories engendered within me—this was the other key—and I wasn't sure that feeling could be conjured later on merely by depressing the "play" button. So I had to work quickly while the interview was fresh in my head. My goal, therefore, was to produce on the page, however possible, both my subject's voice and my emotional response. To the extent I have done that the book succeeds. If I haven't then it fails, irrespective of how true to the raw audio the words on the page may be.

What is truth? That's a sticky wicket. Truth, of course, is honesty and accuracy, but it's a cop-out to stop there and say that we always know what that means. Setting aside politics for the moment, are we so sure we know what's honest and accurate at all times and in all situations? I could have done what Ritter claimed to be doing and present the oral histories largely as transcribed, but would that have been an honest, accurate, and truthful representation? Ritter clearly didn't think so and neither do I. I don't know why Ritter was so hesitant to reveal his process, but one thing I wanted to make sure to do here was not repeat what I consider to be the one glaring error of the otherwise flawless *The Glory of Their Times*. So I'm going to tell you what I did.

First, I didn't hesitate to rearrange the text in order to conform to a roughly chronological progression of events within a player's narrative. While I did try to progress through my interviews in chronological fashion, my subjects and I often went offtrack, veering here and there, and then returning, sometimes hours later, to a topic raised early on. My intent in speaking with my subjects was to pose general questions pointing them in the direction of their upbringing, their stay in this Minor League town or that one, and then let them talk.

Some of the players I spoke with seemed to have a deep well of stories they were just bursting to tell; I got the impression more than once that these stories were bottled up inside of them and held there for decades because they didn't believe that anybody cared (several players confessed at some point during our conversations that the stories they were telling were ones they'd either never told before or only to their immediate families). Given an audience at last they set them free, one after another. In the process, chronology took a holiday as they veered from a recollection of their early childhood to something that occurred while they were in, say, the Midwest League, and then back again. When this occurred, as it often did, I adjusted my role to be that of keeping track of tales started but abandoned partway through. Toward the end of these interviews I'd review my notes and circle back to those stories in order to learn what happened or how they connected with other recalled events.

Other players were more hesitant to share much more than the basics at first, and understandably so. They didn't know me and I didn't know them; oftentimes I was calling them cold and asking them to reveal some of the most personal and painful stories in their lives to a complete stranger. (Occasionally a player I'd spoken to would refer me to another player he thought might be interested in speaking with me and he'd contact that player on my behalf first, putting in a good word for me and letting him know that I could be trusted. I'm forever in my debt to those players for that act of kindness.) With the more hesitant subjects my method was a bit different: I'd try to start our conversation on a light note and focus on more comfortable topics until I sensed that they were more at ease, at which point I could try to broach the more difficult and personal subjects. Regardless of whether a particular player was loquacious or cautious, however, the resulting transcript would hopscotch every which way. Which made my first order of business in piecing together a narrative obvious: I had to put the jigsaw puzzle together so as to create a recognizable picture out of the countless jagged individual pieces.

Next, I had to figure out what to do with the sentences (as opposed to stories) that tailed off and were never completed. I hadn't realized this before undertaking this project, but once I started paying attention to the dynamics of verbal communication I was astonished at the volume of sentences we start that we never finish. We so often make it about halfway through a point before either cutting ourselves off with a new idea that just came to us, a tangential thought, or simply silence as we either run out of steam or perhaps believe that we've sufficiently made our point such that formally completing it seems superfluous. In the course of a conversation this isn't a problem, but on the page it's death in that it kills the speaker's momentum without mercy and leaves the reader confused, left to sort through the myriad of ideas hanging in the ether. After initially experimenting with preserving these half-thoughts, I found that while they may have been faithful to what was on the recording they were hardly an honest account of the idea being expressed as well as my understanding and reaction to it. Quite frankly, they didn't translate and I decided that to preserve them just so I could say that I preserved them would be an injustice to my subjects and an inaccurate rendering of what they were conveying to me on both an intellectual and emotional level.

So I resolved to complete the thought with words that they didn't utter but which, to borrow Neyer's phrase, I presumed they might have used. In so doing I did my best to not alter the idea being expressed in any way but, rather, to simply complete it such that the impact of the sentence would resonate on the page just as it resonated with me when I heard it. I should add here that I was nervous about doing this—had I jumped a guardrail?—so I made sure to send the completed narratives to my subjects, alerting them to what I'd done and asking them to review the finished product for accuracy.

Specifically, I asked each of them the following: "Please take a look and let me know if I've misstated anything, misunderstood anything, or gotten anything wrong. Please let me know if you don't believe this represents you accurately. It's difficult to translate a spoken conversation into a narrative chapter on the page so I want to make sure that I get it right. If you want to make any changes/corrections/clarifications just let me know and I'll do it."

A few responded with corrections, which I was grateful for. A few said everything looked okay to them. And a few never responded.

Two final points I'd like to make before signing off, the first having to do with the ethics of grammar. Just as we often cut ourselves off when we speak in ways we'd never do when we write, most of us adhere to different grammatical standards in our oral and written communication. We're far looser in our language and conjugation in conversation than we'd ever be at the keyboard. As an oral history presented in the format here requires a translation from the spoken to the written word, I quickly found myself confronted with the question of how to handle the technical grammatical errors represented within the transcripts I was working with. Correct or not to correct? That is the question. Whether 'tis nobler in the mind to suffer the slings and arrows of outrageous conjugation. . . . You get the idea.

After batting this question back and forth I reached a decision that will probably satisfy no one and is, admittedly, perhaps scandalously inconsistent: I concluded that the most honest, the most accurate, the most truthful thing I could do was to correct some of the grammar and leave other grammatical slips alone. As for why, well, sometimes the word on the page, as transcribed from the raw audio, didn't jibe with my emotional response when I heard it spoken in my ear. So I corrected those and if the correction felt more truthful to me I considered that to be the more accurate representation. But other times the corrected grammar felt "off" and gave me the queasy feeling that I was putting words in my subject's mouth that, to use Neyer's standard, I didn't honestly believe he might have used. In those instances I restored the transcribed language. Inconsistent? No doubt. But the truth doesn't always walk a straight line.

My final point involves the inevitable reckoning with the "N-word." In a book such as this it was unavoidable and, obviously, uncomfortable. The subject matter my subjects and I delved into was often difficult and dredged up many powerful memories for the players I spoke with. In expressing them to me that word, as hurled at them from the grandstand or as they were walking down the street, or as an expression of how the condescending and demeaning attitude of a manager or coach made them feel, would sometimes be uttered. Some players used the word itself while others substituted "the N-word" for it. I never asked any of them why they chose one form over the other, but I got the impression that those who used the word itself were doing so to express just how terrible and inhumane a particular experience was for them in the hope that perhaps I could feel—to the extent possible—what they felt, if just a little.

My instinct in those situations was to keep the word in the text, as I had little doubt that it was being utilized for a particular purpose and if my goal was to conjure both my subject's voice and my emotional response, removing it would fail on both counts. Upon reflection, however, I changed my mind. If a player actually said "the N-word" I used that phrase; if he instead used the word itself, I replaced it with a series of asterisks (in this text, two em dashes) following the first letter. As for why I did this, I decided that to include the word might very well result in a diversion of attention from the players' stories to my use of the word in the text. And that would have been a failing more egregious than any other I could possibly make; the last thing I wanted was for this book to focus on me rather than the stories contained within as conveyed by the players who lived them.

I hope this explanatory note on my method has been helpful and that I have succeeded, at least somewhat, in conveying on the page both the voice of the speaker and the palpable effects I experienced while listening to the incredible, funny, sad, tragic, uplifting stories told by people who did me the honor of indulging my questions and curiosity to reveal all that they revealed of their fascinating lives. I am eternally grateful for their willingness to spend some time speaking with me so deeply and openly.

As for my personal evaluation of my effort here, I think I was most successful in achieving all that I hoped to achieve in the "found poetry," as I've come to call it, that begins each player's chapter. I should add that nothing at all was added or rearranged when I wrote in verse; I simply identified the passage within a transcript that moved me most deeply and presented it—as is—on the page. I did add some negative space here and there or group words or phrases together or separately in an effort to convey the texture of what I heard, and in reviewing them now once again believe that the poetic rendering of their verbal prose comes closest to delivering both the power of their voice and the power of the response it engendered within me. As for the chapters that followed, I employed the methods discussed above in order to come as close as possible to what I felt to be the truth.

I guess what I'm trying to say here with all of this is that I tried my best.

Notes

1. Lawrence S. Ritter, *The Glory of Their Times: The Story of the Early Days of Baseball Told by the Men Who Played It* (New York: Harper Perennial, 1966/2010).
2. Ritter, *Glory of Their Times*, xvi.
3. David Lawrence Reed, "Lawrence S. Ritter: The Last New York Giant," SABR *Baseball Research Journal* 33, no. 97 (2004): 98.
4. Ritter, *Glory of Their Times*, xviii.
5. Rob Neyer, *Rob Neyer's Big Book of Baseball Legends* (New York: Fireside, 2008), 146–52.
6. Neyer, *Rob Neyer's Big Book*, 151.
7. Neyer, *Rob Neyer's Big Book*, 148.
8. Neyer, *Rob Neyer's Big Book*, 152.
9. Reed, "Lawrence S. Ritter," 98.
10. Reed, "Lawrence S. Ritter," 98.

APPENDIX
Player Statistics

MICKEY BOWERS

YEAR	AGE	TM	LG	LEV	AFF
1968	19	Huron Phillies	Northern League	A-	PHI
1969	20	Spartanburg Phillies	Western Carolinas League	A	PHI
1969	20	FIL Phillies	Florida Instructional League North	WRk	PHI
1970	21	Peninsula Phillies	Carolina League	A	PHI
1978	29	Alexandria Dukes	Carolina League	A	

MILT KELLY

YEAR	AGE	TM	LG	LEV	AFF
1970	19	Orlando Twins	Florida State League	A	MIN
1971	20	Wisconsin Rapids Twins	Midwest League	A	MIN
1971	20	Lynchburg Twins	Carolina League	A	MIN
1974	23	Petroleros de Poza Rica	Mexican League	AAA	

EDGAR PATE

YEAR	AGE	TM	LG	LEV	AFF
1969	19	Billings Mustangs	Pioneer League	Rk	SEP
1969	19	AIL Pilots	Arizona Instructional League	wRk	SEP
1971	21	Danville Warriors	Midwest League	A	MIL
1971	21	Newark Co-Pilots	New York–Pennsylvania League	A-	MIL
1972	22	Visalia Mets	California League	A	NYM
1973	23	Memphis Blues	Texas League	AA	NYM
1973	23	Visalia Mets	California League	A	NYM
1974	24	Visalia Mets	California League	A	NYM
1975	25	Algodoneros de Union Laguna	Mexican League	AAA	

MOE HILL

YEAR	AGE	TM	LG	LEV	AFF
1965	18	Fox Cities Foxes	Midwest League	A	BAL
1965	18	FIL Orioles	Florida Instructional League	wRk	BAL
1966	19	Batavia Trojans	New York–Pennsylvania League	A	
1966	19	Miami Marlins	Florida State League	A	BAL
1966	19	Stockton Ports	California League	A	BAL
1966	19	FIL Orioles	Florida Instructional League	wRk	BAL
1967	20	Miami Marlins	Florida State League	A	BAL
1968	21	Miami Marlins	Florida State League	A	BAL

APPENDIX 183

1970	23	Orlando Twins	Florida State League	A	MIN
1971	24	Wisconsin Rapids Twins	Midwest League	A	MIN
1971	24	Charlotte Hornets	Dixie Association	AA	MIN
1971	24	Lynchburg Twins	Carolina League	A	MIN
1972	25	Wisconsin Rapids Twins	Midwest League	A	MIN
1973	26	Wisconsin Rapids Twins	Midwest League	A	MIN
1974	27	Wisconsin Rapids Twins	Midwest League	A	MIN
1975	28	Wisconsin Rapids Twins	Midwest League	A	MIN
1976	29	Wisconsin Rapids Twins	Midwest League	A	MIN
1977	30	Wisconsin Rapids Twins	Midwest League	A	MIN
1978	31	Wisconsin Rapids Twins	Midwest League	A	MIN
1979	32	Jacksonville Suns	Southern League	AA	KCR
1980	33	Fort Myers Royals	Florida State League	A	KCR

LEROY REAMS

YEAR	AGE	TM	LG	LEV	AFF
1962	18	Idaho Falls Yankees	Pioneer League	C	NYY
1963	19	Idaho Falls Yankees	Pioneer League	A	NYY
1964	20	Eugene Emeralds	Northwest League	A	PHI
1965	21	Chattanooga Lookouts	Southern League	AA	PHI

LEROY REAMS (cont.)

YEAR	AGE	TM	LG	LEV	AFF
1966	22	Macon Peaches	Southern League	AA	PHI
1966	22	San Diego Padres	Pacific Coast League	AAA	PHI
1967	23	Reading Phillies	Eastern League	AA	PHI
1968	24	Reading Phillies	Eastern League	AA	PHI
1969	25	Reading Phillies	Eastern League	AA	PHI
1969	25	Eugene Emeralds	Pacific Coast League	AAA	PHI
1969	25	Philadelphia Phillies	National League	Maj	PHI
1970	26	Montgomery Rebels	Southern League	AA	DET
1970	26	Toledo Mud Hens	International League	AAA	DET

AARON POINTER

YEAR	AGE	TM	LG	LEV	AFF
1961	19	Houston Buffs	American Association	AAA	CHC
1961	19	Salisbury Braves	Western Carolina League	D	
1962	20	Durham Bulls	Carolina League	B	HOU
1962	20	Oklahoma City 89ers	American Association	AAA	HOU
1963	21	San Antonio Bullets	Texas League	AA	HOU
1963	21	Houston Colt .45s	National League	Maj	HOU
1964	22	San Antonio Bullets	Texas League	AA	HOU
1965	23	Amarillo Sonics	Texas League	AA	HOU

966	24	Oklahoma City 89ers	Pacific Coast League	AAA	HOU
1966	24	Houston Astros	National League	Maj	HOU
1967	25	Oklahoma City 89ers	Pacific Coast League	AAA	HOU
1967	25	Houston Astros	National League	Maj	HOU
1968	26	Tacoma Cubs	Pacific Coast League	AAA	CHC
1968	26	Oklahoma City 89ers	Pacific Coast League	AAA	HOU
1969	27	Tacoma Cubs	Pacific Coast League	AAA	CHC
1970	28	Nishitetsu Lions	Japan Pacific League	Fgn	
1971	29	Nishitetsu Lions	Japan Pacific League	Fgn	
1972	30	Nishitetsu Lions	Japan Pacific League	Fgn	

RON ALLEN

YEAR	AGE	TM	LG	LEV	AFF
1964	20	Miami Marlins	Florida State League	A	PHI
1965	21	Miami Marlins	Florida State League	A	PHI
1966	22	Tidewater Tides	Carolina League	A	PHI
1966	22	Spartanburg Phillies	Western Carolinas League	A	PHI
1967	23	Tidewater Tides	Carolina League	A	PHI
1968	24	Reading Phillies	Eastern League	AA	PHI
1969	25	Reading Phillies	Eastern League	AA	PHI
1970	26	Tidewater Tides	International League	AAA	NYM
1970	26	Memphis Blues	Texas League	AA	NYM
1971	27	Tidewater Tides	International League	AAA	NYM

RON ALLEN (cont.)

YEAR	AGE	TM	LG	LEV	AFF
1972	28	Tulsa Oilers	American Association	AAA	STL
1972	28	St. Louis Cardinals	National League	Maj	STL

ROBERT KELLY

YEAR	AGE	TM	LG	LEV	AFF
1965	20	Spartanburg Phillies	Western Carolinas League	A	PHI
1966	21	Spartanburg Phillies	Western Carolinas League	A	PHI
1967	22	Spartanburg Phillies	Western Carolinas League	A	PHI
1968	23	Tidewater Tides	Carolina League	A	PHI
1969	24	Reading Phillies	Eastern League	AA	PHI
1969	24	FIL Phillies	Florida Instructional League North	WRk	PHI
1970	25	Reading Phillies	Eastern League	AA	PHI
1970	25	Eugene Emeralds	Pacific Coast League	AAA	PHI
1971	26	Eugene Emeralds	Pacific Coast League	AAA	PHI
1971	26	Reading Phillies	Eastern League	AA	PHI
1972	27	Eugene Emeralds	Pacific Coast League	AAA	PHI
1973	28	Rocky Mount Phillies	Carolina League	A	PHI
1973	28	Petroleros de Poza Rica	Mexican League	AAA	
1974	29	Petroleros de Poza Rica	Mexican League	AAA	

| 1975 | 30 | Petroleros de Poza Rica | Mexican League | AAA | |

ROLAND HARDSON

YEAR	AGE	TM	LG	LEV	AFF
1974	21	Lewiston Broncs	Northwest League	A-	OAK

JOHN THOMPSON

YEAR	AGE	TM	LG	LEV	AFF
1969	21	Winnipeg Goldeyes	Northern League	A-	KCR
1970	22	Waterloo Royals	Midwest League	A	KCR
1971	23	San Jose Bees	California League	A	KCR

GLENN STERLING

As of publication, no published statistics were available.

WIL AARON

YEAR	AGE	TM	LG	LEV	AFF
1971	19	Bluefield Orioles	Appalachian League	Rk	BAL
1972	20	Lodi Orions	California League	A	BAL
1973	21	Asheville Orioles	Southern League	AA	BAL
1973	21	Lodi Lions	California League	A	BAL
1974	22	San Antonio Brewers	Texas League	AA	CLE
1975	23	San Antonio Brewers	Texas League	AA	CLE
1976	24	San Jose Bees	California League	A	CLE
1976	24	Williamsport Tomahawks	Eastern League	AA	CLE

CHUCK STONE

YEAR	AGE	TM	LG	LEV	AFF
1971	22	Lakeland Tigers	Florida State League	A	DET
1972	23	Clinton Pilots	Midwest League	A	DET